Herausgeber: Dr. Frank Haß

Blue | Red | Orange Line 1
Förderausgabe

Ernst Klett Verlag
Stuttgart · Leipzig · Dortmund

Inhalt

	Kompetenzziele, Ich kann … | Themen	Seite
Zoom in	Zahlen bis 12 | Farben | Sich vorstellen | ABC	4
Unit 1	**School life**	
Check in	… meine Schule vorstellen.	10
Station 1	… Aufforderungen und Bitten ausdrücken. Schulsachen | Redemittel für den Unterricht	12
Listening	… Anweisungen in der Schule verstehen. Verschiedene Orte an einer Schule	17
Station 2	… über meinen Unterricht sprechen. Wochentage | Schulfächer	18
Viewing	… einen Imagefilm über eine Schule verstehen.	23
Reading	… eine Fotostory verstehen.	24
Check out	Task: Ein Schulvideo	26
Discover	More than lessons	27
Unit 2	**Family and home**	
Check in	… sagen, wie ich wohne.	28
Station 1	… meine Familie vorstellen. Familie	30
Viewing	… einen Vlog über ein besonderes Haus verstehen. Räume zu Hause	35
Station 2	… mein Zimmer beschreiben. Möbel und Gegenstände	36
Listening	… Radiowerbung verstehen.	41
Reading	… einen Comic verstehen.	42
Check out	Task: Ein Spiel	44
Discover	At home with the royal family	45
Unit 3	**Daily life**	
Check in	… über meinen Alltag sprechen.	46
Station 1	… meine Freizeitaktivitäten beschreiben. Freizeitbeschäftigungen | Zahlen bis 100	48
Viewing	… ein Erklärvideo zum Thema Zeit verstehen. Uhrzeit	53
Station 2	… über meinen Tagesablauf sprechen. Alltagsroutine	54
Listening	… Bahnhofsdurchsagen verstehen.	59
Reading	… eine Tiergeschichte verstehen.	60
Check out	Task: Eine Umfrage	62
Discover	Crazy about sport	63

	Kompetenzziele, Ich kann … | Themen	Seite
Unit 4	**Where I live**	
Check in	… sagen, wo ich wohne.	64
Station 1	… ein Treffen vereinbaren. Gebäude und Orte	66
Listening	… eine Stadtführung verstehen.	71
Station 2	… einen Weg beschreiben. Wegbeschreibung | Verkehrsmittel	72
Viewing	… eine Doku über Verkehrsmittel verstehen.	77
Reading	… einen Newsticker verstehen.	78
Check out	Task: Ein Audioguide	80
Discover	A walk around town	81
Unit 5	**Around the year**	
Check in	… über Jahreszeiten sprechen.	82
Station 1	… über das vergangene Jahr sprechen. Monate | Datum	84
Viewing	… eine Reportage verstehen.	89
Station 2	… einen Tagebucheintrag schreiben. Wetter | Ereignisse	90
Listening	… Interviews verstehen.	95
Reading	… eine Legende verstehen.	96
Check out	Task: Ein Jahrbuch	98
Discover	Let's celebrate!	99
Unit 6	**Out and about**	
Check in	… Ausflugsziele benennen.	100
Station 1	… mich über Ausflüge unterhalten. Dinge und Personen beschreiben	102
Listening	… ein Hörspiel verstehen.	107
Station 2	… Essen und Trinken bestellen. Lebensmittel | Mengenangaben	108
Viewing	… eine Videoanleitung zu Rezepten verstehen.	113
Reading	… Infotexte verstehen.	114
Check out	Task: Ein Quiz	116
Discover	Six must-see places	117
	Anhang	Seite
V	**Vocabulary**	
	Vokabeln in Wortfeldern	118
	Wörterbuch Englisch – Deutsch	133

Welcome!

Elliot Nisha

 1 Sing the welcome song. ▶ Vokabeln Seite 118 (V1-2)
A 1   Singe das Willkommenslied.

10 – 9 – 8 – 7 – 6 – 5 – 4 – 3 – 2 – 1 – Hello!

Blue, blue, blue is the colour of your shoes,
Red, red, red is the colour of your hat,
White, white, white is the colour of your shirt,
Green, green, green is the colour of your dress.

One, two, three, come with me,
Four, five, six, a colour mix,
Seven, eight, nine, you look so fine,
Ten, I like you!
Welcome to England!
Welcome to Greenwich!

Brown, brown, brown is the colour of your hair,
Grey, grey, grey is the colour of your skirt,
Black, black, black is the colour of your top,
Pink, pink, pink is the colour of your cap.

One, two, three, …

10 – 9 – 8 – 7 – 6 – 5 – 4 – 3 – 2 – 1 – zero!

Zoom in

Katie
Joshua

2 Find all the numbers in … Finde alle Zahlen in … ▶ Vokabeln Seite 118 (V1-2)

1. blue   🟦   2, 8
2. _____   🟥   _____
3. _____   🟩   _____
4. _____   ☁   _____
5. _____   🟨   _____

1 7 8 10
      5
   6   4
0   2 9 3

3 Hello

a) Read the dialogue between Nisha and Katie.
Lies das Gespräch zwischen Nisha und Katie.

Nisha	Hi, my name is Nisha. What's your name?
Katie	Hi Nisha, my name is Katie.
Nisha	Nice to meet you. How are you?
Katie	Great.
Nisha	See you later!
Katie	Bye!

Say hi
Hi! – Hello!
Say bye
Bye! – Goodbye!
See you later!

b) Say hello to a partner like Nisha and Katie.
Begrüße deinen Partner oder deine Partnerin wie Nisha und Katie.

You   Hi, my name is …
Your partner   Hello … , I'm …

5

Zoom in

 4 Sing the alphabet song.

Singt das Alphabet-Lied.

A, B, C, D, E, F, G, H, I, J, K, L, M, N, O, P, Q, R, S, T, U, V, W, X, Y and Z.

A is for apple. 	B is for bear. 	C is a candle and also a chair. 
D is for dog. 	E is for eggs. 	F is a frog that has green legs. 
G gorilla, 	H ham, 	I iguana, 
J jam. 	K is a king. 	L, he's a lion. 
M is a mouse – hey look! He's a Mayan. 	N is a needle, 	O the ocean, 
P is a pig with a magic potion. 	Q is a queen, 	R is a rat, 
S is a snake, 	T Take that!	U an umbrella, 
V violin. 	W is the water – let's all jump in! 	X is a xylophone. 
Y is a yak. 	Z is a zebra, which brings us back to . . . 	

5 New students

a) Listen and read the dialogue. Hör zu und lies das Gespräch.

Naomi	Hi, what's your name?
Harry	I'm Harry .
Naomi	Pardon, can you spell that, please?
Harry	H – A – R – R – Y
Naomi	Ah, Harry . Thank you.

b) Spell your names to each other. Look at page 6 for help.
Buchstabiert einander eure Namen. Hilfe findest du auf Seite 6.

6 Talk to a partner about yourself. Sprich mit jemandem über dich.

Naomi	Hi, Harry . How old are you?
Harry	I'm eleven . And you?
Naomi	I'm twelve .
Harry	Where are you from?
Naomi	I'm from Greenwich . And you?
Harry	I'm from Brighton .

Hi, I'm Emmy. What's your name?

Setzt an den farbigen Stellen eure eigenen Namen , euer Alter und euren Wohnort ein

7 Make your name card. Bastel dein Namensschild.

Zoom in

8 The games

An vielen Stellen im Buch findest du grüne Symbole. Diese stehen für einen Link zu einem Video oder einem Audio. Die Links brauchst du, um die Übung zu lösen. Du brauchst dazu ein Handy, ein Tablet oder einen PC.

Finde heraus, was die Symbole bedeuten, und setze ein Häkchen bei der richtigen Antwort. Ihr könnt es auch zu zweit machen. Die Buchstaben <u>vor</u> der jeweils richtigen Antwort ergeben das Lösungswort.

Hier finde ich:

▶ einen Film
V 2
- C über Emmy. ☐
- H mit Elliot. ☐
- M über den Weg zur Thomas Tallis School. ☐

▶ einen Film über
V 7
- E verschiedene Zeiten. ☐
- Z Skateboards. ☐
- J Bowlingkugeln. ☐

Zoom in

 einen Hörtext über
A 5
- A Katzen. ☐
- L Schulsachen. ☐
- O die Thomas Tallis School. ☐

 einen Hörtext über
A 11
- L eine Tasche. ☐
- D einen Ball. ☐
- P eine Jacke. ☐

 ein Lied über
A 15
- L eine Wette. ☐
- G ein Sportteam. ☐
- O ein Familie. ☐

Das Lösungswort lautet: _____

1 School life

Am Ende dieser Unit kann ich ...
- meine Schule vorstellen.
- Aufforderungen und Bitten ausdrücken.
- Anweisungen in der Schule verstehen.
- über meinen Unterricht sprechen.
- einen Imagefilm über eine Schule verstehen.
- eine Fotostory verstehen.

A

I'm Elliot.
I go to Thomas Tallis School.
I'm in **Year 7**.
My **school uniform** is blue and grey.
It's OK.

B My **tutor** is Mr Turner.

C My **English teacher** is Mrs Bashir.

D My **friends** are Josh and Harry.

Culture

Thomas Tallis School, kurz TTS, ist eine Schule im Londoner Stadtteil Greenwich. Die Schule ist nach einem englischen Komponisten benannt. Wie heißt deine Schule? Woher kommt der Name?

Check in 1

1 Who can you see in the photos? Complete the sentences.
Wen kannst du auf den Fotos sehen? Vervollständige die Sätze.

students   teacher   tutor ✓

I can see a   *tutor*   in photo B.

I can see a   _____   in photos B and C.

I can see   _____   in photos A and D.

2 Match the classroom phrases with their German meaning.
Verbinde die Sätze mit ihrer deutschen Bedeutung.

Meine Klassenlehrerin ist Frau …   My English teacher is Mr …

Mein Englischlehrer ist Herr …   My friends are …

Ich bin in der 5. Klasse.   My tutor is Mrs …

Meine Freunde sind …   Meine Schuluniform ist …

My school uniform is …   I'm in Year 5.

3 Your turn: Talk about your school.
Sprecht über eure Schule.

I'm Max . I go to Albert Schweitzer-Schule .   …
I'm in Year 5 .
My tutor is Mr Baier .   Ms   Mrs
My English teacher is Mrs Hartmann .
My friends are Daniel and Erhan .

> Du kannst diesen Text als Mustertext nehmen und einzelne Wörter austauschen.

✓ Ich kann meine Schule vorstellen.

Station 1

At Thomas Tallis School

1 Read the text. Lies den Text.

Mr Turner	Good morning boys and girls. My name is Mr Turner. **Look at the board**, please.
Katie	Excuse me, **can you help me**, please?
Mr Turner	Yes, of course.
Katie	Is this Mrs Turner's class?
Mr Turner	This is Mr Turner's class. I'm Mr Turner. **Sit down**, please.
Katie	Hi Nisha, nice to see you!
Mr Turner	**Be quiet**, please. **Listen to me** and **don't talk.**
Katie	Sorry, Mr Turner.

> **Culture**
> In England tragen die Schülerinnen und Schüler meistens eine Schuluniform. Wie findest du das?

2 Put in the right words. Setze die richtigen Wörter ein.

| Sit down | Listen | Look ✓ | help |

1. _Look_ at the board, please.

2. S_____, please.

3. Can you h_____ me?

4. L_____ to me.

Station 1

3 Things for school

a) **Listen and say.** Höre zu und sprich nach. ▶ Vokabeln Seite 119 (V5)

seven phones

one tablet

one exercise book

ten folders

three pens

one bag

two books

> Schon gemerkt? Wörter in der Mehrzahl haben am Ende ein **-s**!
> one pen – two pens

b) **Look at the photos again. Listen and point to the right photo.**
Schau dir die Fotos noch einmal an. Höre zu und zeige auf das richtige Foto.

4 How many of these things are in your school bag? Write the numbers.
Wie viele von diesen Sachen hast du in deiner Schultasche?
Schreibe die Zahlen auf.

 _1_ phone

 ___ tablet

 ___ pen

> Ergänze ein **-s** am Ende, wenn du mehr als einen dieser Gegenstände hast.

 ___ exercise book

 ___ folder

 ___ book

1 Station 1

5 Talk about things in your school bags. ▶ Vokabeln Seite 119 (V5)
Sprecht über Dinge in euren Schultaschen.

A Can I have your pen , please?

B Yes, of course.   B Sorry, no.
A Thank you.   A That's OK.

> **Culture**
> Menschen in England sagen ganz oft *please*, *sorry* und *thank you*. Wie ist das in deiner Sprache?

6 Tick the sentence that matches the picture.
Setz ein Häkchen bei dem Satz, der zum Bild passt.

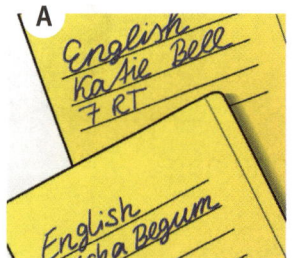

A
a) Can you sit down, please? ☐
b) Can you open your folders, please? ✓

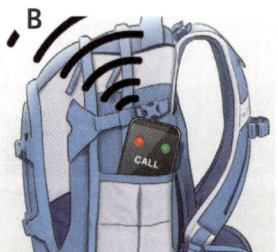

B
a) Can you write that on the board, please? ☐
b) Can I take out my phone, please? ☐

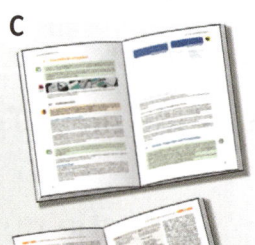

C
a) Can you close your books, please? ☐
b) Can you be quiet, please? ☐

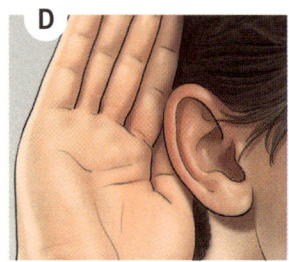

D
a) Can I have your pen, please? ☐
b) Can you say that again, please? ☐

7 Talk to each other. Unterhaltet euch.

A Can you close your books , please?
B Yes, of course.

open your folders

say that again

write that on the board

Station 1 1

Language

So bittest du jemanden, etwas zu tun oder etwas nicht zu tun:

Open your book, please. **Öffne** dein Buch.
Don't open your book. **Öffne** dein Buch **nicht**.

Look at the board, please.

8 What can you say? Write a sentence for each picture.
Was kannst du sagen? Schreibe einen Satz zu jedem Bild.

Open your book, please. ✓   Look at the board, please.   Don't talk.

Take out your book, please.   Don't sit down.

A

B

C
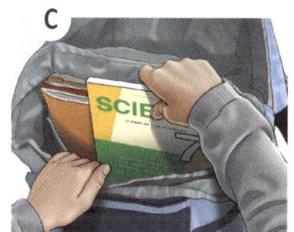

Open your book, please.

D

E

9 Play the game. Spielt das Spiel.

Eine Person gibt Befehle auf Englisch. Führe nur die Befehle aus, in denen *please* vorkommt. Machst du einen Fehler, bist du raus.

Sit down, please.   Sit down.

1 Station 1

10 Your turn: Can you help me, please?
Practise different situations in the classroom.
Übe verschiedene Situationen im Klassenraum.

Step 1: Read the role cards. Lies die Rollenkarten.

A

Student A Dein Stift schreibt nicht mehr. Frage jemanden, ob du einen Stift haben kannst.
Student B Gib ihm oder ihr einen Stift und sage: „Ja, natürlich."

B

Student A Du warst in der letzten Stunde nicht da. Frage jemanden, ob du seinen oder ihren Ordner ansehen kannst.
Student B Gib ihm oder ihr deinen Ordner und sage: „Hier ist mein Ordner."

C

Student A Du hast nicht verstanden, was deine Lehrerin oder dein Lehrer gesagt hat.
Teacher „Ja, natürlich."

Step 2: Which situation is it? Write the right letter.
Welche Situation ist es? Schreibe den richtigen Buchstaben auf.

Can you say that again, please?   –   Yes, of course.   Dialogue [C]

Can I have your pen, please?   –   Yes, of course.   Dialogue [ ]

Can I look at your folder, please?   –   Here is my folder.   Dialogue [ ]

Step 3: Make dialogues. Swap roles.
Unterhaltet euch. Tauscht die Rollen.

✓ Ich kann Aufforderungen und Bitten ausdrücken.

School rules

1 Places at school

a) Write the places at school under the right photos. ▶ Vokabeln Seite 119 (V6)
Schreibe die Schulorte unter die richtigen Fotos.

classroom   playground   cafeteria ✓   toilet   library   gym   office

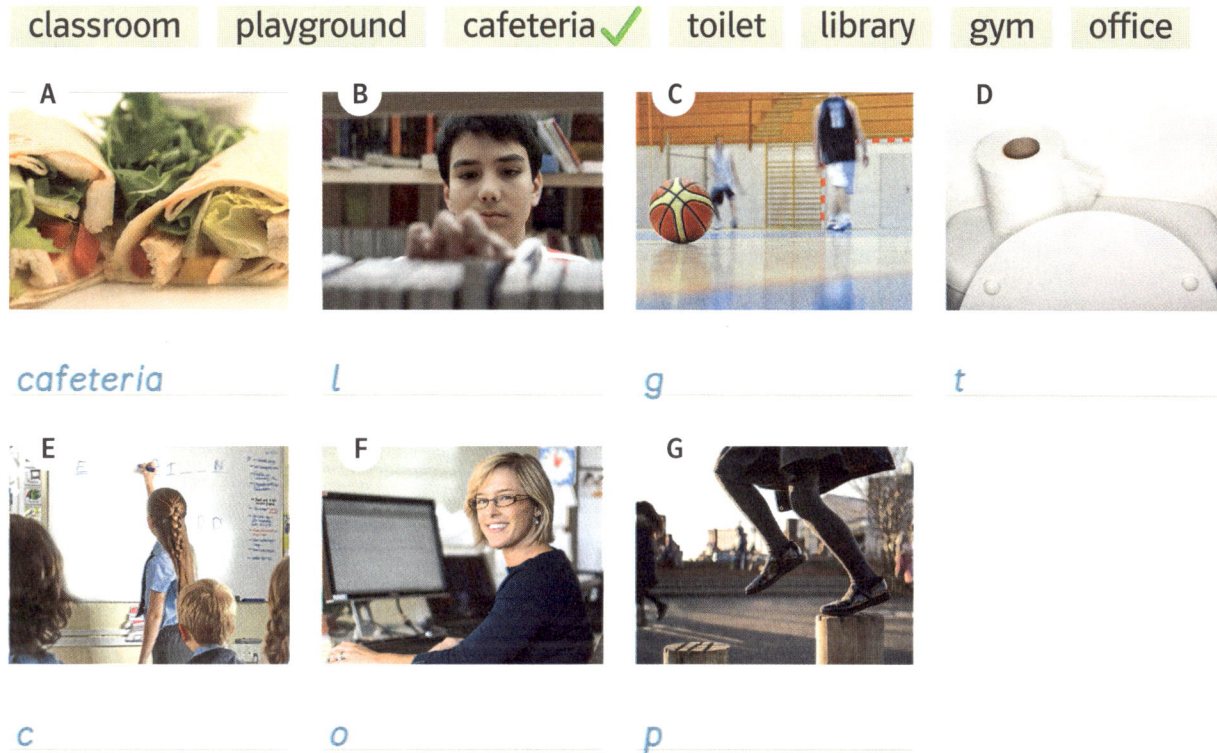

A cafeteria   B l_____   C g_____   D t_____

E c_____   F o_____   G p_____

🔊 **b) Listen and say. Point to the right photos.**
A 7   Hör zu und sprich nach. Zeige auf die richtigen Fotos.

🔊 **2 Listen and find out the places from exercise 1.**
A 8   Hör zu und finde heraus, welche Orte von Übung 1 gemeint sind.

3 Choose two school rules. Draw symbols for them.
Wähle zwei Schulregeln aus. Zeichne Symbole dafür.

No bags.

No phones.

Listen to me.

Be quiet.

✓ Ich kann Anweisungen in der Schule verstehen.

1 Station 2

School days

1 Read the text. Lies den Text.

Nisha	Hi Katie.
Katie	Hi Nisha. I like this school.
Nisha	**Science** is my favourite subject. I like **maths** too. And you?
Katie	My favourite subjects are **English** and **art**.
Nisha	Art is OK, but English is difficult. I don't like Wednesday – we have **PE**. It's boring.
Katie	I like PE. It's easy. Science is difficult.
Nisha	I can help you with your science homework and you can help me with English.
Katie	Cool!

2 Who likes what? Tick the right subject.
Wer mag was? Setze Häkchen bei den richtigen Schulfächern.

science?

☐ Katie ✓ Nisha

maths?

☐ Katie ☐ Nisha

English?

☐ Katie ☐ Nisha

art?

☐ Katie ☐ Nisha

PE?

☐ Katie ☐ Nisha

Station 2

3 Listen and do the chant. Höre zu und wiederhole den Sprechgesang.

History and music,
Tutor time and art.
Go to registration,
Then the day can start.
(Chorus) It's a school mix.
It's a school mix.

Go into the playground,
See your friend at break.
In the cafeteria,
Sandwiches and cake.
(Chorus) It's a school mix.
It's a school mix.

4 Match the school subjects with the right photos. ► Vokabeln Seite 120 (V8)
Ordne die Schulfächer den richtigen Fotos zu.

history   geography ✓   IT   biology

Im Englischen schreibst du die meisten Wörter klein. Sprachen *(English, German, …)* und Wochentage *(Monday, …)* schreibst du groß.

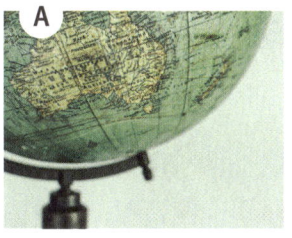
A

B

C

D

geography   b   h

5 Days of the week ► Vokabeln Seite 120 (V7)

a) Listen and say the days of the week.
Höre zu und sprich die Wochentage nach.

Monday – Tuesday – Wednesday – Thursday – Friday – Saturday – Sunday

b) Put the days of the week in the right order.
Bringe die Wochentage in die richtige Reihenfolge.

☐   ☐   1   ☐   ☐   ☐   ☐

Station 2

Language

So beschreibst du Menschen und Sachen:
I am ten. **Ich bin** zehn.
You are my friend. **Du bist** mein Freund.
She is nice. **Sie ist** nett.
It is an old book. **Es ist** ein altes Buch.
We are friends. **Wir sind** Freunde.
You are smart. **Ihr seid** clever.
They are in my class. **Sie sind** in meiner Klasse.

„You" heißt „du" (Einzahl) und „ihr" (Mehrzahl).

6 Tick the right small word. Kreuze das richtige kleine Wort an.

1. a boy   a) he ✓
            b) they ☐

2. Mrs Bashir   a) you ☐
                b) she ☐

3. the school   a) she ☐
              b) it ☐

4. you and I   a) we ☐
              b) they ☐

5. you and Katie   a) she ☐
                   b) you ☐

6. the lessons   a) they ☐
               b) it ☐

7 Complete Nisha's sentences with <u>is</u> or <u>are</u>.
Vervollständige Nishas Sätze mit <u>is</u> oder <u>are</u>.

1. My school *is* TTS.
2. Katie and Harry _____ in my class.
3. My teachers _____ OK.
4. Mr Turner _____ my science teacher.
5. My favourite day _____ Wednesday.
6. My favourite subjects _____ science and maths.

Für Gegenstände und Tiere ohne Namen benutzt man immer *it*.

8 Long forms and short forms

a) Read Elliot's email.
Underline the short forms.
Lies Elliots E-Mail.
Unterstreiche die Kurzformen.

> I am – I'm
> you are – you're
> it is – it's
> Die Kurzformen werden vor allem beim Sprechen oder bei persönlichen Nachrichten, z. B. an Freunde, verwendet.

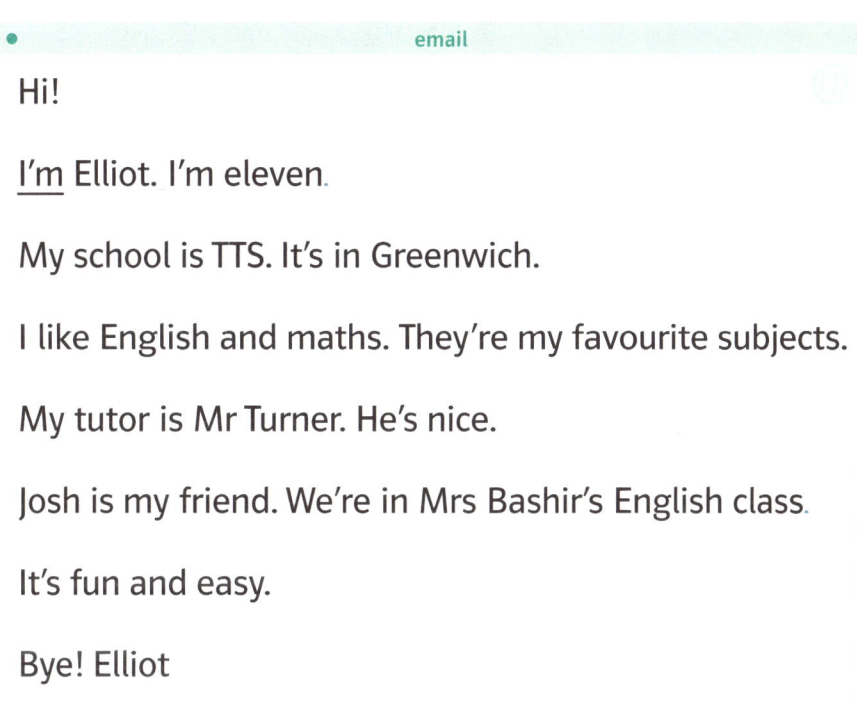

Hi!

I'm Elliot. I'm eleven.

My school is TTS. It's in Greenwich.

I like English and maths. They're my favourite subjects.

My tutor is Mr Turner. He's nice.

Josh is my friend. We're in Mrs Bashir's English class.

It's fun and easy.

Bye! Elliot

b) Write the underlined short forms from exercise a) in the table.
Schreibe die Kurzformen, die du in a) unterstrichen hast, in die Tabelle.

Einzahl			Mehrzahl		
Langform	Kurzform		Langform	Kurzform	
I am		ich bin	we are		wir sind
you are	you're	du bist	you are	you're	ihr seid
he is		er ist	they are		sie sind
she is	she's	sie ist			
it is		es ist			

1 Station 2

9 Your turn: My lessons
Make a timetable and talk about your lessons at school.
Mache einen Stundenplan und sprich über deine Schulstunden.

Step 1: Tick your subjects. ▶ Vokabeln Seite 120 (V8)
Setze Häkchen bei deinen Schulfächern.

- ☐ English
- ☐ German
- ☐ maths
- ☐ PE
- ☐ art
- ☐ music
- ☐ biology
- ☐ IT

Step 2: Make a timetable. Schreibe einen Stundenplan.

Class 5a

	Monday	Tuesday	Wednesday	Thursday	Friday
1					
2					
3					
4					

Step 3: Write about your lessons. Schreibe über deine Schulstunden.

My favourite subject is art .   maths   English   PE   …

It's on Thursday and Friday .   Monday   Tuesday   Wednesday

My teacher is Mr / Mrs … .   …

He's / She's nice .   cool   OK   great   interesting

Step 4: Practise your sentences. Übe deine Sätze.

Step 5: Present your text. Präsentiere deinen Text.

✓ Ich kann über meinen Unterricht sprechen.

A tour of TTS

1 Match the phrases with the right photos.
Ordne die Ausdrücke den richtigen Fotos zu.

do PE   have lunch   find a book

A  B  C

find a

2 Watch the film. Put the photos in the right order.
Schau dir den Film an. Setze die Fotos in die richtige Reihenfolge.

A  B C  D

library   cafeteria   gym   playground

3 Match the correct sentence parts. Verbinde die richtigen Satzteile.

Students can find a book — in the cafeteria.

Students can talk to friends — in the recording studio.

Students can have lunch — in the library.

Students can do PE — in the playground.

Students can make films and music — in the gym.

 Ich kann einen Imagefilm über eine Schule verstehen.

1 Reading

My bag!

Katie Hi, Nisha. I can't find my bag. Can you help me?
Nisha Yes, of course.

Katie Look! That's my bag! Hey! You on the bike! Stop!
Nisha That's Elliot.

Katie Elliot!
Elliot Yes. Can I help you?
Katie That's my bag! My books and tablet are in it.

Elliot This is my bag. Look! Here are my books and my lunchbox.
Katie Oh, I'm sorry.

Elliot Can I help you find your bag, Katie?

Joshua Elliot! Your bag!
Elliot My bag?!?
Katie Oh, that's **my** bag. Thank you, Josh.

Reading 1

1 Who or what can you see in the photos? Complete the sentences.
Wen oder was kannst du auf den Fotos sehen? Vervollständige die Sätze.

Katie | Nisha ✓ | Elliot | Joshua | TTS | his bag

A: I can see *Nisha* and Katie.

B: Nisha and Katie are at _____.

C: I can see Katie and _____.

D: I can see Katie with Elliot and _____.

E: I can see Elliot, Katie and _____ with a blue bag.

F: I can see _____, Nisha, Elliot and Joshua.

2 Read the text. Lies den Text.

3 Read the story to the class.
Lies die Geschichte der Klasse vor.

1. Bildet Gruppen von vier Personen.
2. Such dir aus, ob du Katie, Nisha, Elliot oder Joshua vorlesen möchtest.
3. Übe deinen Text.
4. Lest die Geschichte zusammen vor.

Skills

Du übernimmst die Rolle einer Person im Text. Lies die Sätze der Person mehrmals laut vor. Überleg dir auch, ob du selbst schon mal so etwas erlebt hast. Wie war das für dich?

4 Play the game: Whose bag is it? ▶ Vokabeln Seite 118 (V2)
Spielt das Spiel: Wem gehört die Tasche?
Eine Person beschreibt eine Schultasche im Raum. Die anderen müssen raten, wem sie gehört.

Student A I can see a **blue** bag .   green   red and white   …
Student B Is it Tim's bag?
Student A No.
Student C Is it Emma's bag?

✓ Ich kann eine Fotostory verstehen.

1 Check out

Task: My school video

Bildet Gruppen. Erstellt ein Video, das etwa eine Minute dauert. Präsentiert es in der Klasse.

Step 1: Find rooms or places at your school. ▶ Vokabeln Seite 119 (V6)
1. Erstellt eine Liste von wichtigen Räumen oder Orten an eurer Schule.
2. Wählt einen Ort für euer Video aus.

Step 2: Write your text.
1. Sag Hallo, nenne den Namen deiner Schule und wo und wer ihr seid.
2. Sag noch ein oder zwei Sätze zu jedem Ort.
3. Verabschiede dich zum Schluss.
4. Überprüfe deinen Text.

> Hello. This is the Schillerschule in Frankfurt. We are class 5a. This is our cafeteria. It's nice.
>
> Bye!

Step 3: Plan your video.
1. Wählt einen Sprecher oder eine Sprecherin und eine Kameraperson aus.
2. Benutzt euer Handy oder eine Kamera, um die Szenen zu filmen.
3. Wählt einen Kameraort aus.

> **Media tip**
> Es ist einfacher, wenn ihr einen festen Standort wählt. Den Text kann eine Person vor oder hinter der Kamera sprechen.

Step 4: Make the video.
1. Übt den Text, bevor ihr anfangt.
2. Filmt die Szenen.
3. Schaut euch das Video an. Kann man alles gut sehen? Kann man alles verstehen? Wenn nicht, filmt die Szene noch einmal.

Step 5: Show the video in class. Zeigt das Video in der Klasse.

Discover 1

More than lessons

1 Look at the photos and talk about the clubs.
Schau dir die Fotos an und sprich über die AGs.

netball

computer club

orchestra

drama

coding and robots

rowing

A Netball – that's cool.   OK   boring
B I like drama.

2 Talk about your school clubs.
Sprich über deine Schul-AGs.

Our school clubs are hip hop, …   football   badminton   table tennis
I go to the computer club .   …
It's cool .   fun   nice
It's on Friday .   Monday   Tuesday   Wednesday   …

2 Family and home

Am Ende dieser Unit kann ich …
- sagen, wie ich wohne.
- meine Familie vorstellen.
- einen Vlog über ein besonderes Haus verstehen.
- mein Zimmer beschreiben.
- Radiowerbung verstehen.
- einen Comic verstehen.

A

B

I live in a **house** in Brook Lane.

C
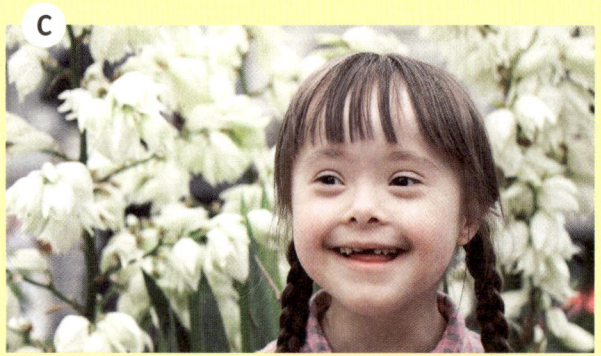
I live there with my **mum** and my **sister** Kira. I have my own room. I don't have a **brother**.

D

Milo is our cat.

E

My **dad**'s **flat** is in Greenwich too.
I share a room with my sister there.

Culture
Englische Adressen sehen so aus:
Katie Bell
125 Brook Lane
London SE3 0EB
Worin unterscheiden sich deutsche Adressen?

Check in 2

1 Words for family and home

a) Complete the mind maps. Vervollständige die Mindmaps.

flat ✓   sister   house   mum ✓   dad   room   brother

mum _____   flat _____

(family)   (home)

b) Complete the sentences. Vervollständige die Sätze.   share   my own

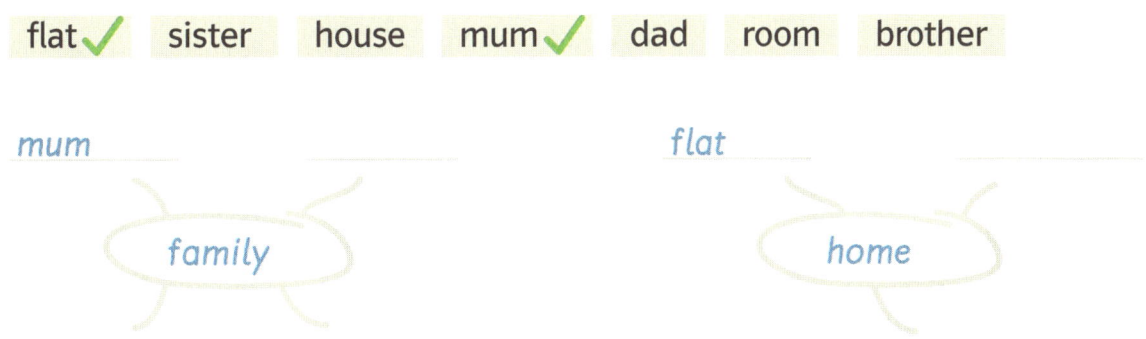

I have _____ room.   I _____ my room.

2 Draw a mind map of your own family. ▶ Vokabeln Seite 121 (V9)
Zeichne eine Mindmap deiner eigenen Familie.

3 Your turn: Talk about where you live.
Sprecht darüber, wo ihr wohnt.
▶ Vokabeln Seite 121

Du kannst diesen Text als Muster nehmen und deine eigenen Wörter einsetzen.

My name is … .

I live in a flat in Frankfurt .   house
                                         Wedel   Chemnitz   …

I live with my mum and my sister .   brother   dad   dog

I share a room with my sister ./   …
I have my own room.

It's nice .   great   OK   big   …

✓ Ich kann sagen, wie ich wohne.

2 Station 1

Joshua and his family

1 Read the text. Lies den Text. ▶ Vokabeln Seite 121 (V9)

A This is my grandpa Osaro. He's funny.

B This is my sister. Her name is Yola. She's OK.

C My brother Noam is cool. He's 15 years old.

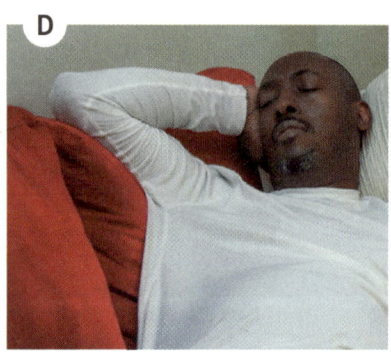

D My dad is very quiet.

E This is my mum, and this is my grandma Ada. They're great.

F This is my grandpa's dog, Rocky. He's a good dog, but he's crazy. I like him.

2 Complete the sentences. Vervollständige die Sätze.

dad | sister | mum and grandma | brother | grandpa ✓ | dog

1. Joshua's *grandpa* is funny.
2. Joshua's *s*_____ is OK.
3. Joshua's *b*_____ is cool.
4. Joshua's *d*_____ is quiet.
5. Joshua's *m*_____ are great.
6. Grandpa's *d*_____ is crazy.

Station 1 2

3 Listen and say.

a) Listen and say the words. ► Vokabeln Seite 121 (V9)
A 12
Hör zu und sprich die Wörter nach.

father – mother – brother – with – another

Nimm die Zungenspitze ganz leicht zwischen die Zähne und summe.

b) Listen and say the sentence.
A 13
Höre zu und sprich den Satz nach.

Father, mother, sister, brother – hand in hand with one another.

4 Joshua's cousins

a) Listen and read. Höre zu und lies mit. ► Vokabeln Seite 121 (V9)
A 14

Joshua
Look at the photos.
These are my <u>cousins</u>, Prince and Kelvin.
They have no sisters.
Their <u>parents</u> are Sakita and Aren.
Sakita is my <u>aunt</u>, and Aren is my <u>uncle</u>.
Our <u>grandparents</u> are Osaro and Ada.

b) Match the underlined words with their German meaning.
Verbinde die oben unterstrichenen Wörter mit ihrer deutschen Bedeutung.

cousins   Tante

parents   Großeltern

aunt   Cousins

uncle   Eltern

grandparents   Onkel

Skills
Du kannst die Wörter hinten im Buch oder in einem Online-Wörterbuch nachschlagen.

2 Station 1

5 Mediation

Joshua hat einen kurzen Text über seine Familie geschrieben. Während du den Text liest, fragt deine kleine Schwester, worum es darin geht. Beantworte die Fragen auf Deutsch. Die hervorgehobenen Wörter können dir helfen.

Culture

Joshuas Nachname Numa kommt aus Nigeria. Er kann Vorname oder Nachname sein. Er bedeutet „schön" oder „angenehm". Was bedeutet dein Nachname?

> document
>
> I have a big family. My <u>grandparents</u> are from <u>Nigeria</u>. I have a <u>brother</u> and a <u>sister</u>. We live in Greenwich with my <u>parents</u>. My <u>cousins</u> live in Southwark. That's a part of <u>London</u> too. I like them. My <u>aunt</u> and my <u>uncle</u> are nice too.

1. Wer gehört zu Joshuas Familie? Zu Joshuas Familie gehören _____ .

2. Woher kommen Joshuas Großeltern? Sie kommen aus _____ .

3. Wo wohnt Joshuas Familie? Sie wohnen alle in _____ .

6 Sing the family song. Singt das Familienlied.
A 15

This is my dad, football is his game,
This is my mum, she's a music fan.
This is my brother, he's a crazy kid.
Together we are a family.

We're in the garden, everyone is here,
Mum and Dad and my brother too.
We live here, our name is on the door.
Together we are a family.

(Chorus)
Mum and Dad, my brother and me,
This is my family.
Mum and Dad, my brother and me,
Together we are a family.

Hey, it's my friend!
Hi, come in and meet my family!
Hi, nice to meet you! Hello there!

Station 1 **2**

> **Language**
> So sagst du, wie oder was jemand oder eine Sache **nicht ist.**
> I'm **not** Emmy. Ich bin **nicht** Emmy.
> He **isn't** here. Er **ist nicht** hier.
> They **aren't** new. Sie **sind nicht** neu.

Life isn't easy in Greenwich.

7 Find the pairs and write down the hidden word.
Finde die Paare und schreibe das versteckte Wort auf.

1. I am not		R	he isn't
2. you are not		T	we aren't
3. he is not		N	it isn't
4. she is not		P	I'm not
5. it is not		S	they aren't
6. we are not		A	you aren't
7. they are not		E	she isn't

Lösungswort: P ☐ ☐ ☐ ☐ ☐ ☐

8 Write sentences about you and your family.
Schreibe Sätze über dich und deine Familie.

1. My parents **are** | **aren't** cool.   *My parents are cool.*
2. **I'm** | **I'm not** nine years old.   _____
3. My favourite colour **is** | **isn't** grey.   _____
4. **We're** | **We aren't** from London.   _____
5. Our flat/house **is** | **isn't** new.   _____

2 Station 1

9 Your turn: My family
Talk about your own family. You can use photos or draw pictures.
Sprich über deine eigene Familie. Du kannst Fotos nehmen oder Bilder malen.

Step 1: Find a photo or draw a picture for each family member.
Finde ein Foto oder male von jedem Familienmitglied ein Bild.

Step 2: Make a family tree.
Erstelle einen Familienstammbaum:
1. Ordne deine Fotos oder Bilder auf einem Poster an.
2. Schreibe die Namen und ziehe Linien mit einem Bleistift und einem Lineal.
3. Prüfe deinen Familienstammbaum. Stimmt alles?
4. Klebe die Fotos oder Bilder jetzt auf. Benutze einen gut sichtbaren Stift, wenn du die Linien und Namen nachzeichnest.

Step 3: Write about your family. Schreibe über deine Familie.

This is my family.

This is my mum . She's OK .   dad   sister   grandpa   …

This is my brother Tim.   funny   great   cheeky   …

He's 15 years old . He's cool .

This is my grandma . She's very old .

We aren't a big family.   are

Step 4: Practise your text. Then show your family tree to your group and talk about your family.
Übe deinen Text. Dann zeige deinen Stammbaum deiner Gruppe und sprecht über eure Familien.

Ich kann meine Familie vorstellen.

A small house

1 Watch the film. Which places are in the film? Tick. ▶ Vokabeln Seite 122 (V10)
Schau dir den Film an. Welche Orte kommen in dem Film vor? Setze Häkchen.

A ✓ kitchen   B ☐ garden   C ☐ living room

D ☐ bedroom   E ☐ bathroom   F ☐ dining room

2 Watch the film again and choose the right answer.
Schau dir den Film noch einmal an und wähle die richtige Antwort aus.

1. It's a house for   ✓ two people.   ☐ a big family.
2. The house is   ☐ black and yellow.   ☐ green and brown.
3. The bedroom is   ☐ white.   ☐ grey.
4. It's a house with ☐ three rooms.   ☐ four rooms.
5. You can see a   ☐ dog in the garden. ☐ cat in the garden.

3 Talk about your own house. Sprich über dein eigenes Zuhause.

We have a `kitchen` , … .   `living room` `bathroom` `…`

My bedroom is `white` and `…` .   `pink` `yellow` `blue` `…`

My favourite room is the `…` .

✓ Ich kann einen Vlog über ein besonderes Haus verstehen.

Station 2

Katie's home

1 Read the text. Lies den Text. ▶ Vokabeln Seite 123

The Bells are at home. They can't find Milo, the family's cat. Where is he?

Mum Katie, where's Milo? He isn't **under** the sofa.
Katie Is he **on** the table in the kitchen?
Mum No, he isn't there. Milo!
Ah, there you are.
Katie, Milo is in your bedroom now. Close the door!
Katie OK, Mum. Milo, where are you? Are you on the shelf? No.
Are you under the bed? No. Are you **in** a box?
Mum, where are his snacks? Are they in the kitchen?
Mum Yes, they are.
Katie Milo! Where are you? Let's go, Kira. Let's find Milo!

2 Complete the sentences. Vervollständige die Sätze.

on   behind   next to   in front of ✓   under

in front of the door

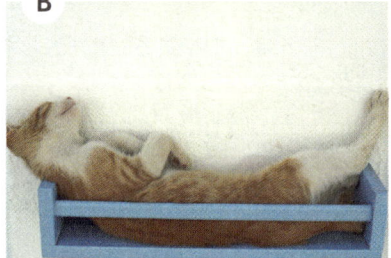
o_____ the shelf

u_____ the table

b_____ the tablet

n_____ the dog

Hier kommt Hilfe!
on auf
behind hinter
next to neben
in front of vor
under unter

Station 2 2

3 Write these things in the right place. ▶ Vokabeln Seite 123 (V11)
Schreibe diese Dinge an die richtige Stelle.

bed   table   shelf   box   lamp   cupboard   bin ✓   picture   chair   window

1. bin
2. l
3. t
4. ch
5. b
6. s
7. cu
8. b
9. w
10. p

Sieh dir das Bild genau an. Wo hat sich Milo versteckt?

Milo is in the c ☐ ☐ ☐ ☐ ☐ ☐ ,
in a b ☐ ☐ .

2 Station 2

Language

Bei Fragen wandern **is** (= **ist**) und
are (= **bist** und **sind**) an den Anfang:

Mum is at home.   You are at home.

Is Mum at home?   Are you at home?

4 Find a classmate for each question who says yes.

Findet für jede Frage jemanden, der oder die mit ja antwortet.

Im Englischen ist es unhöflich, nur mit *Yes* oder *No* zu antworten.

1. Are you eleven?   – Yes, I am. | No, I'm not.
2. Are you good at English?   – Yes, I am. | No, I'm not.
3. Is your favourite animal a cat?   – Yes, it is. | No, it isn't.
4. Is your home a flat?   – Yes, it is. | No, it isn't.
5. Is your favourite place your bedroom?   – Yes, it is. | No, it isn't.

5 Look at Kira's table and ask questions. Find five differences.

▶ Vokabeln Seite 123 (V11)

Seht euch Kiras Tisch an und stellt Fragen. Findet fünf Unterschiede.

A

B

A Is there a book on Kira's table?   B Yes, there is. / No, there isn't.
A Are there …   B Yes, there are. / No, there aren't.
A …   B …

Station 2

6 Match each question with 2 photos. Ordne jeder Frage 2 Fotos zu.

1. What is that?   *A and*

2. Who is that?

3. Where is Milo?

> So einfach ist das:
> **What** is that?   Was ist das? (Sache)
> **Who** is that?   Wer ist das? (Person)
> **Where** is Milo?   Wo ist Milo? (Ort)

It's a bed.

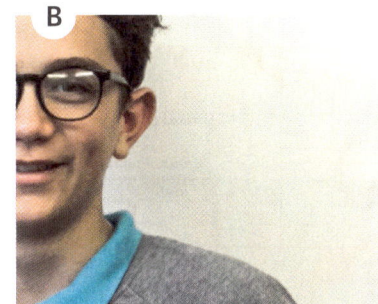

It's Elliot.

He's on the sofa.

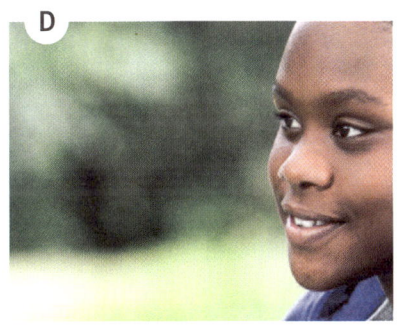

It's Joshua.

He's in a box.

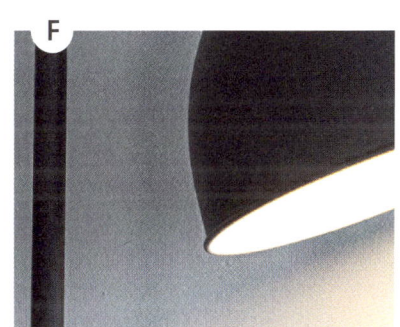

It's a lamp.

7 Connect the parts. Then ask and answer the questions.
Verbindet die Satzteile. Dann stellt Fragen und beantwortet sie.

Where are —————————— your bedroom?

Is your home ——————— you from?

What's your favourite   your family?

What colour is   a flat?

Who are   room?

> What's = What is

8 Your turn: My room

Step 1: Choose 3 pieces of furniture. ▶ Vokabeln Seite 123 (V11)
Wähle 3 Möbelstücke aus.

Step 2: Choose 3 other things. Wähle 3 andere Dinge aus.

Step 3: Draw your room.
Don't show it to your partner.
Zeichne dein Zimmer. Zeige es nicht
deinem Partner oder deiner Partnerin.

Step 4: Ask questions about your partner's room.
Stelle Fragen zum Zimmer deines Partners oder deiner Partnerin.

A Is there a sofa in your room?   table   chair   cupboard   shelf

B Yes, there is. / No, there isn't.

A Is there a book in your room?   lamp   bag   bin   box

B Yes, there is. / No, there isn't.

A Where is the book ?

B It's on the sofa .   in   under   next to   behind
in front of

Step 5: Swap roles. Tauscht die Rollen.

✓ Ich kann mein Zimmer beschreiben.

New things for your home

1 Radio ads

a) Write the correct word under each photo.
Schreibe das richtige Wort unter jedes Bild.

phone   lamp ✓   school bag   pens   chair   book

lamp

b) Listen to the radio ads and match them with the photos.
Höre dir die Radiowerbung an und ordne sie den Bildern zu.

A 16

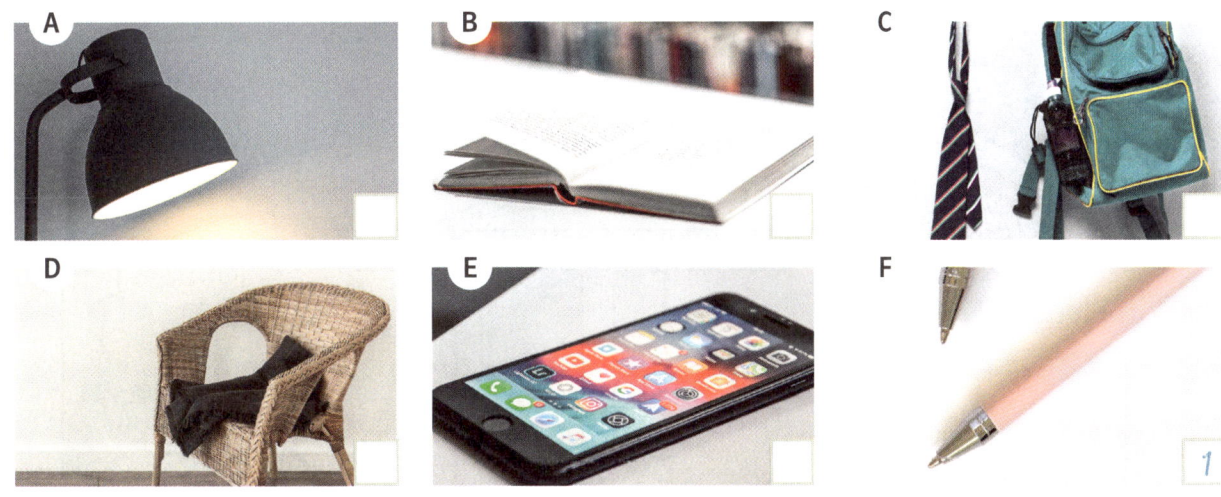

✓ Ich kann Radiowerbung verstehen.

2 Reading

It's not funny, Dad! – Es ist nicht witzig, Papa!

Aidan's parents are not at home.

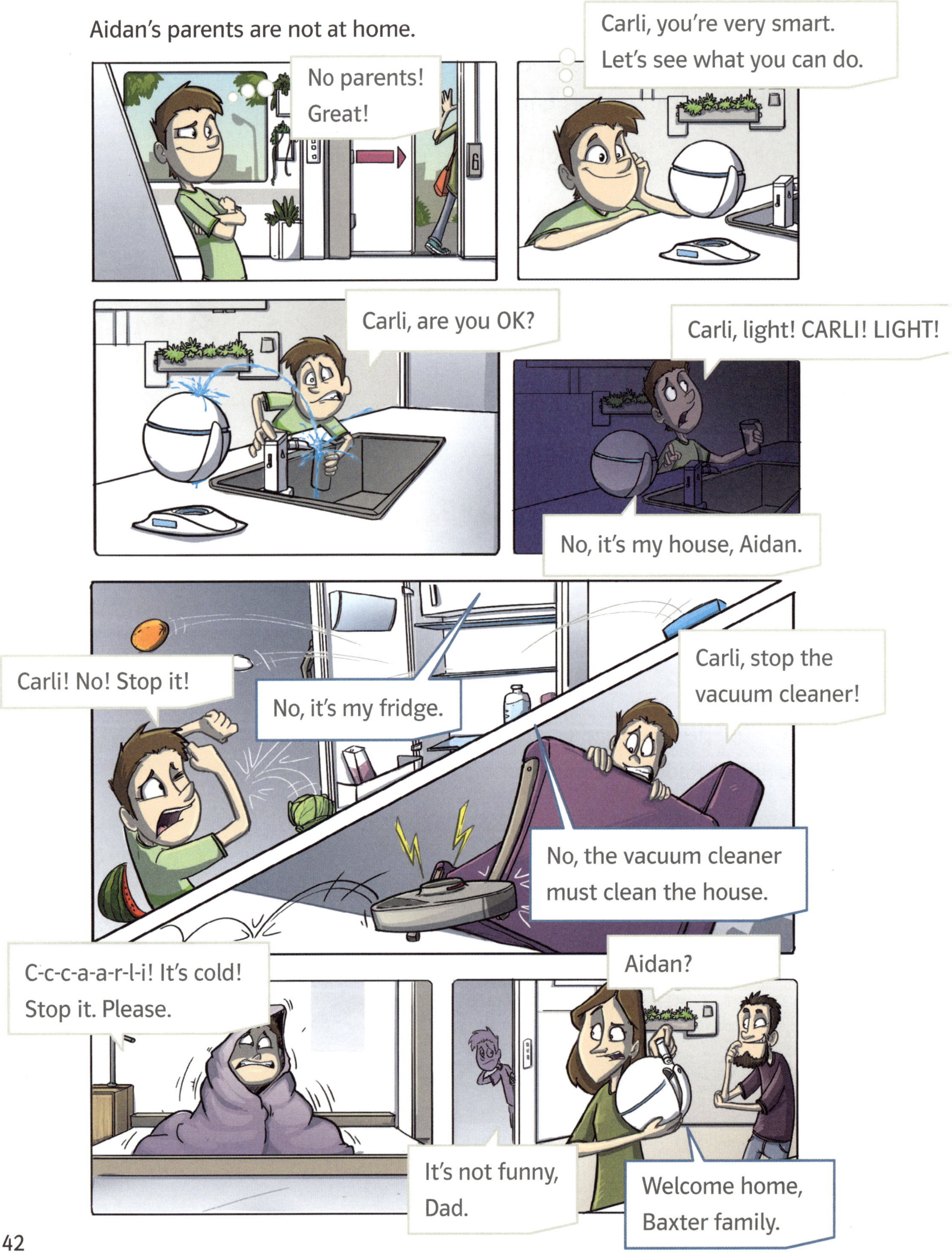

Reading 2

1 Read the text. Lies den Text.

2 Read the text again. Who says it? Is it Aidan or Carli?
Lies den Text noch einmal. Wer sagt das? Ist es Aidan oder Carli?

1. „Are you OK?"
2. „It's my house."
3. „Light!"
4. „Welcome home!"
5. „I'm cold."
6. „Stop it!"

3 Find the right English words and do the crossword.
Finde die richtigen englischen Wörter und löse das Kreuzworträtsel.

smart   funny   light   cold   kitchen ✓   parents   fridge

1. Küche
2. Kühlschrank
3. clever
4. kalt
5. Licht
6. Eltern
7. witzig

✓ Ich kann einen Comic verstehen.

2 Check out

Task: A family game – Ein Familienspiel

Stell dir vor, du bist eine dieser Personen auf dem Bild. Nimm eine Sprachnachricht auf. Können die anderen erraten, wer du bist?

Step 1: Lies die Sprachnachrichten. Wer ist es?

A
I'm Anna. I'm 70 years old. I live with Sam and our cat Harry. I love books. The living room is my favourite place.

B
I'm Robert. I'm 45 years old. I live with Paul and Sarah in a small house. They are 12 and 15 years old. I work at home.

C
I'm Mike. I'm 40 years old. We are the Mayer family. Our dog Ben is crazy. My favourite room is the kitchen.

`man in house number 1`   `man in house number 5`

`grandma in house number 3`

A It's the _____

B It's the _____

C It's the _____

Step 2: Wähle eine Sprachnachricht aus und übe den Text.

Step 3: Nimm die Sprachnachricht auf. Benutze dein Handy oder einen Computer mit Mikrofon.

Step 4: Spiele deine Sprachnachricht der Klasse vor. Können die anderen erraten, wer es ist?

Media tip

Hast du langsam und deutlich gesprochen? Ist die Aussprache richtig? Ist die Aufnahme frei von Störgeräuschen?

At home with the royal family
Zu Hause bei der königlichen Familie

The royal family are England's most famous family. They have many homes. One of them is Windsor Castle in Berkshire.
Let's go on a tour.

Die königliche Familie ist die berühmteste Familie in England. Sie haben viele Häuser. Eins davon ist Windsor Castle in Berkshire.
Lass uns auf eine Tour gehen.

1 Find the place on a map. Finde den Ort auf einer Landkarte.

The Long Walk from the road to Windsor Castle is more than four kilometres long.

This is William and Kate at Buckingham Palace.

This is one of the dining rooms. The castle has about 1,000 rooms.

2 Do you like Windsor Castle? Tick.
Gefällt euch Windsor Castle? Setzt Häkchen.

☐ I like Windsor Castle. The park is great.

☐ I like Windsor Castle. It's very big.

☐ I don't like it. It's too big for me.

☐ I don't like Windsor Castle. It's very old.

☐ I like the dining room. It's cool.

3 Daily life

Am Ende dieser Unit kann ich ...
- über meinen Alltag sprechen.
- meine Freizeitaktivitäten beschreiben.
- ein Erklärvideo zum Thema Zeit verstehen.
- über meinen Tagesablauf sprechen.
- Bahnhofsdurchsagen verstehen.
- eine Tiergeschichte verstehen.

A

B
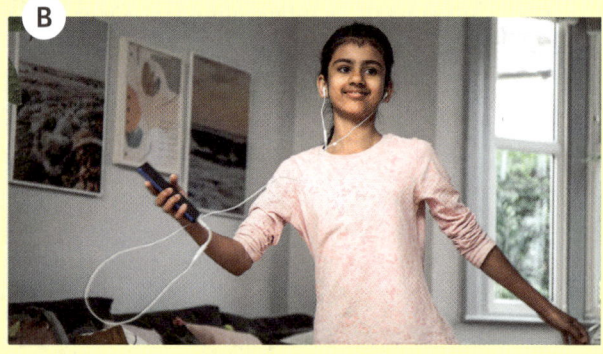

I go to school from Monday to Friday. I like science and the **dance** club.

C

At home we always eat at six o'clock. I **help** in the kitchen in the evenings.

D

I **play** computer games and **watch** football.

E

I don't have a pet, but I often play with my neighbour's dog. That's fun.

Culture

Der Tee ist eines der beliebtesten Getränke in England.
Zur berühmten *teatime* am Nachmittag gibt es Gurkensandwiches und *scones* (süße Brötchen).

Check in 3

1 Activities

a) Match the activities with the photos on page 46.
Ordne die Aktivitäten den Fotos auf Seite 46 zu.

play computer games: That's picture D .

help in the kitchen: That's picture   .

go dancing: That's picture   .

play with the dog: That's picture   .

That's picture   .

Ein Foto bleibt übrig.

b) What are these activities? Wie heißen diese Aktivitäten? ▶ Vokabeln Seite 124

take photos   go shopping ✓   play an instrument   go to the cinema

 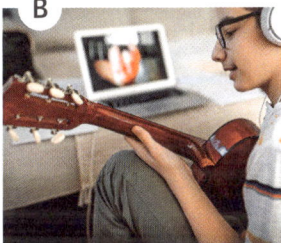  

A   B   C   D

go shopping   p   g   t

2 Your turn: Talk about your activities. Sprecht über eure Aktivitäten.

I go to school from Monday to Friday.

I like maths , but I don't like biology .   English   PE   homework   …

At home I help in the garden .   my mum   my dad   …

I often watch football and I go dancing .   watch films   play games

listen to music   …

✓ Ich kann über meinen Alltag sprechen.

Free-time activities

1 Look at the class survey. Which of these activities do you do?
Sieh dir die Umfrage an. Welche dieser Aktivitäten machst du?

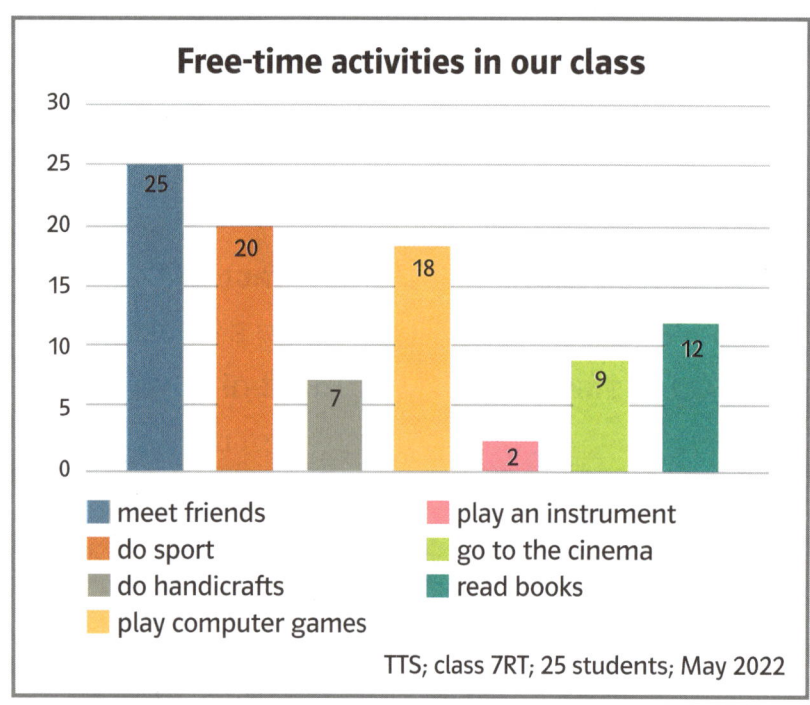

Skills

In einem Säulendiagramm werden Informationen als Säulen dargestellt. Je höher die Säule ist, desto größer ist die Anzahl von etwas.

2 Read the text. Lies den Text.

Elliot Look at our class survey. All 25 students often **meet friends**.
Katie Twenty students **do sport**.
Elliot Eighteen students **play computer games**.
Katie Twelve students **read books**. Nine students **go to the cinema**.
Elliot Seven students **do handicrafts**.
Katie Look, only two students **play an instrument**.
Elliot I often play computer games.
Katie I don't play computer games. I sometimes read books.
Elliot I think we do a lot of things in our free time.

Station 1   3

3 Talk about your free-time activities. ▶ Vokabeln Seite 124 (V12)
Erzählt einander von euren Freizeitaktivitäten.

1. I *often* _____ go shopping.
2. I _____ listen to music.
3. I _____ take photos.
4. I _____ watch films.
5. I _____ repair things.

always	immer
often	oft
sometimes	manchmal
never	nie

4 Listen and say the numbers. ▶ Vokabeln Seite 118 (V3)
A 18

Höre zu und sprich die Zahlen nach.

13	thirteen	52	fifty-two	18	eighteen
24	twenty-four	20	twenty	78	seventy-eight
60	sixty	89	eighty-nine	100	one hundred
33	thirty-three	43	forty-three	15	fifteen
16	sixteen	91	ninety-one		

5 Listen and say. Höre zu und sprich nach.
A 19

A There are nine<u>teen</u> students in our class.
B Nine<u>ty</u> students? In one class?
A No, nine<u>teen</u>.

6 Say and match the next number. Sage die nächste Zahl und ordne sie zu.

1. 10 – 15 – 20 – 25 –   62
2. 8 – 16 – 24 –   30
3. 92 – 82 – 72 –   45
4. 81 – 72 – 63 – 54 –   32

Hier musst du rechnen. Im ersten Beispiel wird immer +5 gerechnet. Was musst du rechnen, um von 8 auf 16 zu kommen?

3 Station 1

> **Language**
>
> So sprichst du über Gewohnheiten:
>
> **I** sometimes listen to music. Ich höre mir manchmal Musik an.
> **You** often watch films. Du guckst oft Filme.
> **They** often meet friends. Sie treffen oft Freunde.
> **We** do a lot of things. Wir tun viele Sachen.
>
> Bei *he, she* und *it* fügst du ein **-s** an das Verb hinzu:
>
> **He** always **repairs** our bikes. **Er** repariert immer unsere Fahrräder.
> **She** often **takes** photos. **Sie** macht oft Fotos.
> **It** never **gets** boring. **Es** wird nie langweilig.

7 Connect the sentence parts. Verbinde die Satzteile.

1. I — do sport.
2. My dad? He — plays games.
3. My mum? She — read books.
4. You and me? We — listens to music.
5. My grandparents? They — meet friends.

> Es gibt mehrere richtige Lösungen. Achte auf das **-s** am Ende der Verben!

8 Add the correct ending where necessary.
Ergänze die richtige Endung, wo du sie brauchst.

1. I always read ___ books.
2. My dad like *s* music.
3. We sometimes go ___ to the cinema.
4. My mum do *s* handicrafts.
5. My sister often go *s* shopping.
6. My brothers never watch ___ old films.

> I, you, we, they: he, she, it:
> go → go**es**
> do → do**es**
> watch → watch**es**
> Achte auf das zusätzliche **-e-** und die Aussprache.

Station 1   3

> **Language**
> Mit *don't* oder *doesn't* sagst du, was man nicht tut:
> I **don't** play football. Ich **spiele nicht** Fußball.
> Dad **doesn't** go swimming. Papa **geht nicht** schwimmen.

9 Complete Joshua's sentences.
Vervollständige Joshuas Sätze.

| doesn't do | don't repair ✓ | don't have | doesn't like |

1. My friends *don't repair* things. (nicht reparieren)
2. I _____ a pet. (nicht haben)
3. My friend Nisha _____ handicrafts. (nicht tun)
4. Grandpa's dog Rocky _____ cats. (nicht mögen)

10 Correct the rumours. Use <u>don't</u> or <u>doesn't</u>.
Korrigiere die Gerüchte. Benutze <u>don't</u> oder <u>doesn't</u>

1. Katie and Nisha listen to music in class. – No, they *don't* _____.
2. Noam goes dancing with Katie. – No, he _____.
3. Elliot and Joshua play computer games at school. – No, they _____.
4. Katie has 14 cats. – No, she _____.

11 Write about you and your partner.
Schreibe über dich und deinen Partner oder deine Partnerin.

I play football .   go swimming   listen to music   …

Emma plays football too.   goes swimming   meets friends   …

Emma and me, we don't play games .   don't have a cat / dog
                                     don't like old films   …

3 Station 1

12 Your turn: My free time
Write a text about your free-time activities. ▶ Vokabeln Seite 124 (V12)
Schreibe einen Text über deine Freizeitaktivitäten.

Step 1: Collect words and phrases. Here are some ideas.
Sammle Wörter und Ausdrücke. Hier sind ein paar Ideen.

- what you do after school   play football   meet friends   do sport
- what you do at the weekend   read books   watch films   play games
- what you don't do   don't go shopping   don't repair things

  don't play an instrument

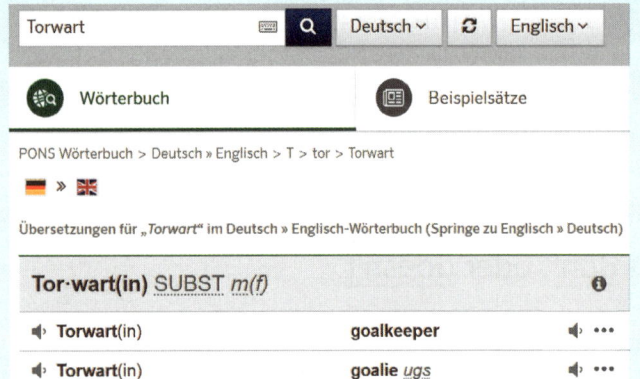

Skills

Möchtest du ein Wort nachschlagen kannst du zum Beispiel ein Online-Wörterbuch benutzen. Dort tippst du das Wort ein und es zeigt dir die Übersetzung.

Step 2: Write 5 sentences for your text. You can use this text as a model.
Schreibe 5 Sätze für deinen Text. Du kannst diesen Text als Vorlage benutzen.

My free time
I often meet my friends after school.
I like sport. I go to the football club.
We often have football games at the weekend.
I don't play an instrument and I don't like handicrafts .

Step 3: Check your spelling and correct it. You can ask for help.
Prüfe, ob du alles richtig geschrieben hast. Du kannst auch um Hilfe bitten.

 Step 4: Present your texts in your group.
Präsentiert eure Texte in eurer Gruppe.

✓ Ich kann meine Freizeitaktivitäten beschreiben.

Viewing 3

What time is it?

1 Write the times under the pictures. ▶ Vokabeln Seite 125 (V13)
Schreibe die Uhrzeiten unter die Bilder.

| nine thirty | six oh five | one forty-five | seven fifteen ✓ |

| eleven o'clock | three fifty |

A **7:15**   B **9:30**   C **11:00**

seven fifteen

C **1:45**   D **3:50**   E **6:05**

2 Watch the film. Tick the right times.
V 7 Schau dir den Film an. Setze ein Häkchen bei den richtigen Zeiten.

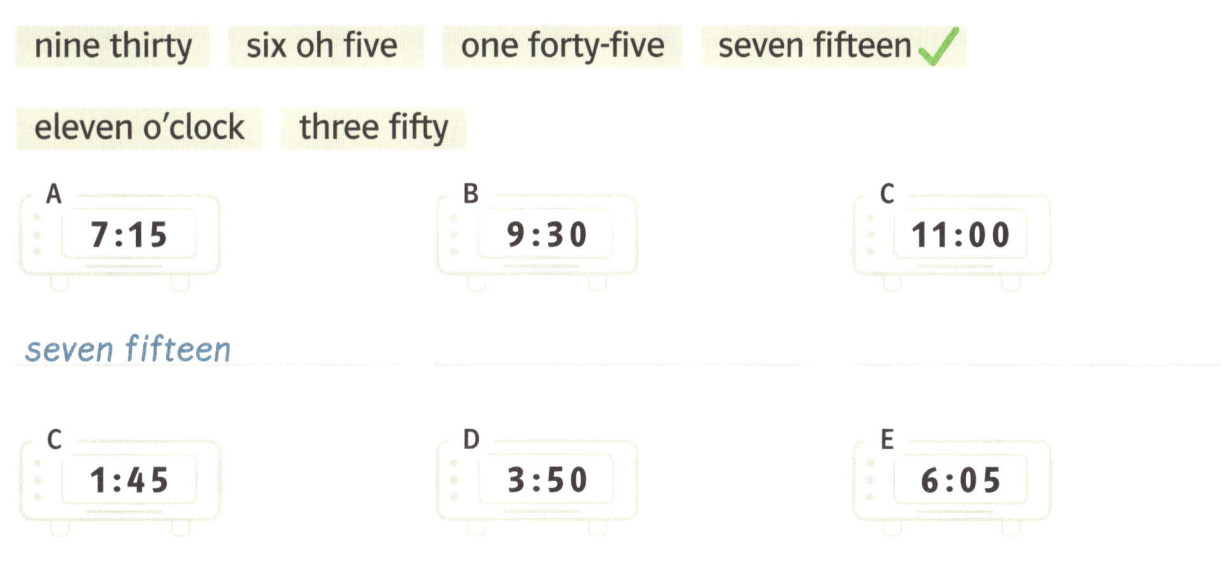

A — New York, at night   B — New York, in the morning   C — Greenwich, dinner time

It's 7:00. ☐   2:00. ☐   It's 7:15. ☐   10:00. ☐   It's 6:30. ☐   7:00. ☐

3 Match the numbers with the right times.
Verbinde die Zahlen mit der richtigen Zeit.

1. 6:30   eight twenty   4. 3:10   eleven thirty-seven
2. 3:45   six thirty   5. 11:37   nine o'clock
3. 8:20   three forty-five   6. 9:00   three ten

✓ Ich kann ein Erklärvideo zum Thema Zeit verstehen.

Station 2

Daily routines

1 Read the text. Lies den Text.

Nisha Begum is at the Royal Observatory in Greenwich. She talks to astronaut Fiona Jenkins.

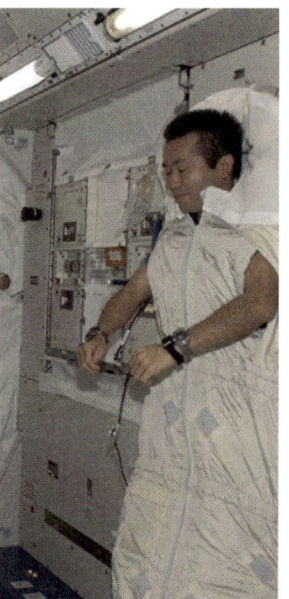

Nisha **When** do you get up at the space station?
Fiona We get up at seven o'clock. Then we have breakfast.
Nisha **What** do you do in the morning?
Fiona We do experiments and talk to people on Earth, then we clean the bathroom or the kitchen.
Nisha **Do you** do sport?
Fiona Yes, we do. I go cycling in the gym every afternoon.
Nisha **When** do you have dinner?
Fiona We have dinner at six o'clock.

2 Put the list about Fiona's day in the right order.
Bringe die Liste über Fionas Tag in die richtige Reihenfolge.

☐ talk to people on Earth	☐ 1 ☐ get up
☐ go cycling	☐ have dinner
☐ have breakfast	☐ clean the kitchen

3 Match the activities from exercise 2 with the pictures.
Ordne die Aktivitäten von Aufgabe 2 den Bildern zu.

talk to p

4 Write down Nisha's daily routine in the right order. ▶ Vokabeln Seite 125 (V14)
Schreibe Nishas Tagesablauf in der richtigen Reihenfolge auf.

12:00 have lunch

8:15 go to school

7:45 have breakfast

7:15 get up

4:30 do homework

6:00 have dinner

10:00 go to bed

Denk dran:
he, she, it –
das **-s** muss mit!

1. Nisha _____ at 7:15. (seven fifteen)
2. She _____ at 7:45. (seven forty-five)
3. Nisha _____ at 8:15. (eight fifteen)
4. She _____ at 12:00. (twelve o'clock)
5. Nisha _____ at 4:30 (four thirty)
6. Nisha _____ at 6:00. (six o'clock)
7. She _____ at 10:00. (ten o'clock)

5 Talk about your daily routines. ▶ Vokabeln Seite 125 (V13–14)
Sprecht über eure täglichen Abläufe.

Student A
I get up at 6:30.
I have breakfast at 6:45.
I go to school at 7:00.
I have lunch at 12:30.
I do my homework at 3:00.
I have dinner at 7:00.
I go to bed at 10:00.

Student B
I get up at 6:00.
I have breakfast at 6:15.
I go to school at 6:45.
I have lunch at 12:30 too.
I do my homework at 5:30.
I have dinner at 7:30.
I go to bed at 9:30.

Setzt überall eure eigenen Uhrzeiten ein.
Wenn du nicht frühstückst, sagst du:
I don't have breakfast.

3 Station 2

Language

So kannst du Fragen stellen und beantworten:

Do you get up at 7:00 every day?
- Yes, I **do**. / No, I **don't**.

Does Lina have a pet?
- Yes, she **does**. / No, she **doesn't**.

6 Ask each other questions and give answers.

Stellt einander Fragen und gebt Antworten.

Student A
1. Do you have a pet?
2. Do you watch films every day?
3. Do you do homework at the weekend?
4. Do you play computer games?
5. Do you help in the garden?
6. Do you repair things at home?

Student B

7 Think of a person in your class. Your partner must guess who it is.

Denke an eine Person in deiner Klasse. Dein Partner oder deine Partnerin muss raten, wer es ist.

Student A			Student B
Does he or she have a pet ?	play computer games		Yes, she does. / No, she doesn't.
	have a brother / a sister		
Does she play football ?	play an instrument	…	Yes, she does. / No, she doesn't.
Is it Sara ?	Tim	…	Yes, it is. / No, it isn't.

Station 2 3

8 Questions for you

a) Complete the questions with the right word.
Vervollständige die Fragen mit dem richtigen Wort.

When   What   Where

What ✓   Where   When

Language
What? = Was?
When? = Wann?
Where? = Wo?

Fragewörter stehen immer am Anfang:
Do you like football?
What do you like?

1. _What_ do you like?
2. _____ do you live?
3. _____ do you do at the weekend?
4. _____ do you get up on Sunday morning?
5. _____ do you go to school?
6. _____ do you do your homework?

Achtung: Bei Verben wie *do sport* oder *do handicrafts* brauchst du bei Fragen zweimal *do*.

b) Ask and answer the questions from a).
Stellt euch die Fragen aus a) und beantwortet sie.

1. I like football .   watching films   dogs   playing games   …
2. I live in Köln .   Wannsee   Vaihingen   …
3. I do sport at the weekend.   clean my room   listen to music   …
4. I get up at 7 o'clock .   at 6:50   at 7:15   at 9 o'clock
5. I go to school at 8:30 .   at 9:30   at 10 o'clock   …
6. I do my homework in the kitchen .   in my room   at school   …

57

3 Station 2

9 Your turn: My day
Talk to your partner about your daily routines. ▶ Vokabeln Seite 125 (V13–14)
Sprecht zu zweit über eure Tagesabläufe.

Step 1: What's your daily routine? Make a schedule. You can use this schedule as a model.
Wie sieht dein Alltag aus? Erstelle einen Zeitplan. Du kannst diesen Zeitplan als Muster benutzen.

My day

Time	What I do
6:45	get up
7:00	have breakfast
7:15	go to school
1:00	have lunch at school
1:30	school or school club
4:00	go home
	do homework
	play games
	on Friday: play football
	…
7:00	dinner
9:30	go to bed

Step 2: Ask a partner. Frage einen Partner oder eine Partnerin.

Student A	Student B
Hi. Can I ask you about your day?	– Yes, of course.
When do you get up?	– I get up at 6:45.
Do you have breakfast?	– Yes, I do./No, I don't.
When do you go to school?	– I go to school at 7:15.
Do you have lunch at school?	– Yes, I do. / No, I don't.
What do you do in the afternoon?	– I do my homework and I play games.
When do you go to bed?	– I go to bed at 9:30.
Thank you. Bye.	– Bye.

✓ Ich kann über meinen Tagesablauf sprechen.

Listening 3

At the train station

1 Match the words with the photos. Ordne die Wörter den Bildern zu.

train | leave | ticket | clean | arrive | train station ✓

ticket office | platform

A — train station
B — t
C — t
D — t

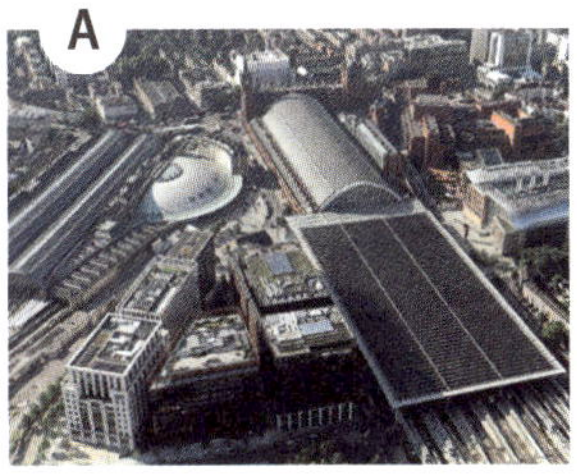

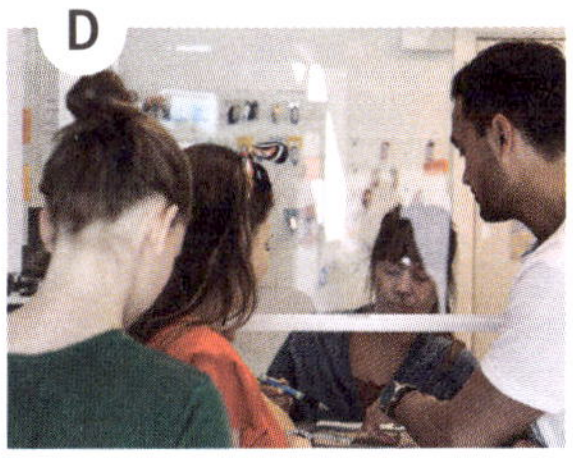

E — a
F — c
G — l
H — p

2 Listen to four announcements and choose the right time.
Höre dir vier Bahnhofsdurchsagen an und wähle die richtige Zeit.

1. When does the train to Birmingham New Street leave?

   A 9:35 ☐   B 10:45 ✓

2. When does the train to Cambridge arrive?

   A 9:10 ☐   B 9:50 ☐

3. When does the ticket office close?

   A 10:00 ☐   B 10:30 ☐

4. When do the toilets close for cleaning?

   A 9.30 ☐   B 3:30 ☐

> Ansagen werden immer wiederholt. Achte dabei nur auf die Information, nach der du gefragt wirst.

✓ Ich kann Bahnhofsdurchsagen verstehen.

3 Reading

A cat's life

A 21

My name is Henry. I live with Lilly Harper and her family in a nice house.

I like my house. My favourite place is my big bed.
Lilly says it's her bed, but it isn't her bed. It's MY bed.
Lily's family often play with me. They're not bad.

It's evening now. Garden time! I miaow[1] and Lilly opens the door.
The neighbour's dog is in my garden!
I get very angry. Silly dog!

Ohh, what's this? It's fish. I love it!

It's 5:30 in the morning. I'm tired and hungry.
I miaow and one of the Harpers opens the door. Time for breakfast.
Where can I sleep today?

1 miaow – *miauen*

A

B

C

D

1 Read the text. Lies den Text.

2 What can you see in the pictures? Tick.
Was kannst du auf den Bildern sehen? Setze ein Häkchen.

In picture A I can see   a black cat. It's Henry. ✓   a brown cat. It's Henry. ☐

In picture B I can see   Henry and a ball. ☐   Henry on a sofa. ☐

In picture C I can see   Henry at breakfast. ☐   Henry and a dog. ☐

In picture D I can see   Henry on a bin. ☐   Henry in a bin. ☐

3 Match the questions with the right answers.
Verbinde die Fragen mit den richtigen Antworten.

1. Who are Henry's family? ——————— the dog
2. What's Henry's favourite place?   at 5:30
3. Who is silly? ——————— Lilly and her family
4. When does Henry go home in the morning?   his big bed

4 Match the words with the photos.
Ordne die Wörter den Bildern zu.   tired   angry

**5 Write 4 sentences about your pet or your dream pet.
Find a photo and present your pet in class.**
Schreibe 4 Sätze über dein Haustier oder dein Traum-Haustier.
Finde ein Foto und präsentiere dein Haustier in deiner Klasse.

This is my dog . Her name is Ilwi .
I always play with her .
She 's a good dog .

✓ Ich kann eine Tiergeschichte verstehen.

3 Check out

Task: A class survey

Do a survey about daily life in your class.
Macht eine Umfrage in eurer Klasse über das tägliche Leben.

Step 1: Bildet Dreiergruppen. Denkt euch 6 Aktivitäten aus. Erstellt eine Tabelle.

Activity	Number of students
1. Do you do sport?	...
2. Do you do your homework?	...
3. Do you help at home?	...
...	...

Step 2: Stellt eure Fragen in der Klasse.
1. Eine/r von euch stellt die Fragen.
2. Eine/r von euch zählt diejenigen, die mit *Yes* antworten.
3. Eine/r von euch schreibt die Anzahl auf.

> Jede Gruppe befragt immer die ganze Klasse auf einmal. Wer mit Ja antwortet, hebt die Hand. Vergesst nicht, eure eigenen Antworten mitzuzählen.

Step 3: Erstellt mit euren Informationen ein Diagramm.

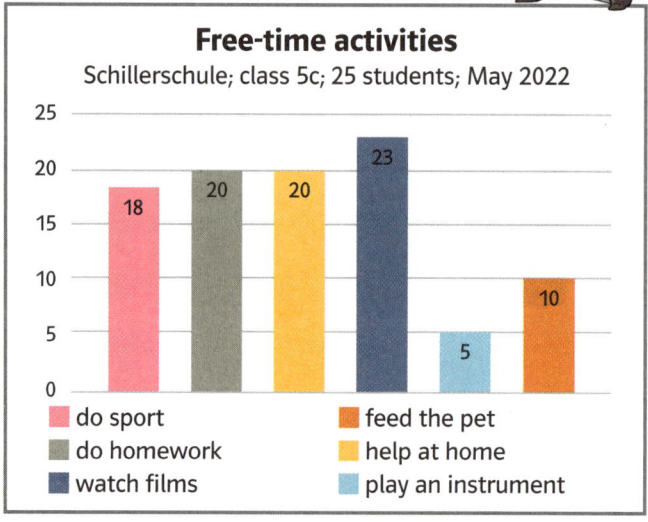

Step 4: Präsentiert eure Ergebnisse in der Klasse.

> *In our class ... students do sport.*
> *... students watch films.*
> *...*

Discover 3

Crazy about sport

1 Which sports do you watch? Which sports do you do?
Welche Sportarten schaust du an? Welche Sportarten machst du?

I watch football .   athletics   tennis   dancing   badminton

I play volleyball .   table tennis   basketball   …

Football: A lot of fans watch football in stadiums or on TV.

Rugby: You play rugby with an oval ball.

Badminton is very popular at schools in England.

Athletics is a group of sports: running, jumping, throwing …

Swimming: Kids in England learn how to swim at school.

Horse racing: The most famous horse racing event is Royal Ascot.

2 Which sports are popular in Germany?
Welche Sportarten sind in Deutschland beliebt?

I think tennis is very popular in Germany.   football   …

Swimming is popular too.   dancing   …

Rugby isn't very popular.   horse racing   …

4 Where I live

Am Ende dieser Unit kann ich …
- sagen, wo ich wohne.
- ein Treffen vereinbaren.
- eine Stadtführung verstehen.
- einen Weg beschreiben.
- eine Doku über Verkehrsmittel verstehen.
- einen Newsticker verstehen.

A

B

I live in Roan Street in Greenwich. It's a part of London.

C

We have a famous **museum**, the Royal Observatory.

D

My friends and I often meet at Cutty Sark. It's an old **ship**.

E

Then we go to the **park** or the **market**. I like Greenwich.

Check in 4

1 Places in town

a) Talk about the photos. Read the sentences and match them with the right photos.
Sprecht über die Fotos. Lies die Sätze und ordne sie den richtigen Fotos zu.

1. I can see Joshua and a ship.   That's picture A .
2. I can see a museum.   That's picture ____.
3. I can see a park and a town.   That's picture ____.
4. I can see Joshua in the street.   That's picture ____.
5. I can see a ship.   That's picture ____.

b) Match the words. Use the right colours. ▶ Vokabeln Seite 126 (V15)
Ordne die Wörter zu. Verwende die richtige Farbe.

famous   market   church   river   street

der Fluss   die Straße   berühmt   der Markt   die Kirche

2 Your turn: Talk about your hometown. Sprich über deinen Heimatort.

I live in Lehmweg in Gifhorn.   Birkenallee   Tonstraße   …

Gifhorn is in Germany.   Würzburg   Münster   …

We have a famous castle and   nice   great   cool   …

an old church.   museum   market   river   …

My town is OK.   village   city

✓ Ich kann sagen, wo ich wohne.

4 Station 1

My town

 1 Look at the map. Which words do you know? ▶ Vokabeln Seite 126 (V15)
Schau dir die Karte an. Welche Wörter kennst du?

1. shop
2. snack bar
3. cinema
4. youth club
5. swimming pool
6. football pitch
7. supermarket
8. library

 2 Listen and point on the map to the places you hear.
Höre zu und zeige auf der Karte auf die Orte, die du hörst.

Station 1   4

3 Name the buildings. Write them. Nenne die Gebäude. Schreibe sie auf.

youth club   snack bar   supermarket

A   B   C

sn _____

4 Listen and say.

a) **Listen and say the words.** Hör zu und sprich die Wörter nach.
A 24

can – cinema – cycling – church

b) **Listen and say the sentence.** Hör zu und sprich den Satz nach.
A 25

You can go cycling and see the church in the city.

5 What can you do at these places? Tick. ▶ Vokabeln Seite 126 (V15)
Was kannst du an diesen Orten tun? Setze ein Häkchen.

A shop   ☐ You can borrow books there.

              ☐ You can buy things there.

A football pitch ☐ You can buy a sandwich there.

              ☐ You can do sport there.

6 Write about your town. Schreibe über deine Stadt.

I live in Helbra.   Neudorf   …

We often go to the youth club.   snack bar   swimming pool   cinema   …

We can play games there.   watch films   go swimming   …

I live in _____

67

4 Station 1

7 Read the phone dialogue. Lies das Telefongespräch.

Katie   Hi Sophie. I'm at the supermarket. Where are you?
Sophie   I'm in the town centre too.
Katie   Can we meet later?
Sophie   Yes, that's a great idea.
            Where do you want to meet?
Katie   Let's meet in front of the new snack bar.
            The sandwiches there are very good.
Sophie   Cool, when?
Katie   In twenty minutes?
Sophie   What about four o'clock?
Katie   OK. See you later.

8 Match the questions with the right answers.
Verbinde die Fragen mit den richtigen Antworten.

Denk dran:
where = wo

1. Where is Katie?   In front of the new snack bar.
2. Where is Sophie?   She's in the town centre.
3. Where do they want to meet?   At four o'clock.
4. What can you eat there?   She's at the supermarket.
5. When do they want to meet?   You can eat sandwiches.

9 Listen and do the chant. Höre zu und mach den Sprechgesang nach.
A 26

In the morning
I go shopping
At the market,
Meet my friend.
We go walking
Down the high street,
Past the snack bar,
Cross the road.

Parks and gardens,
Football pitches,
We can chat or
Play a game.
Cars and taxis,
Bikes and buses,
Always busy,
That's our town!

Station 1 | 4

> **Language**
>
> Im Englischen nennt man den Ort (wo?) **vor** der Zeit (wann?).
> Im Deutschen ist das andersherum:
>
> Let's meet at the snack bar at five o'clock.
>
> Lass uns um 5 Uhr im Café treffen.
>
> I can't go to the museum on Saturday.
>
> Ich kann am Samstag nicht ins Museum gehen.

10 Underline the words and phrases for place and time in different colours.

Unterstreiche die Wörter und Satzteile für Ort und Zeit in verschiedenen Farben.

1. I'm in front of the house now.
2. My friends want to play football in the park in five minutes.
3. We want to watch a film at the cinema in the afternoon.
4. Let's meet next to the library at four o'clock.

11 Talk to each other. Unterhaltet euch.

A Hi Natascha. Can we meet later? ...

B Yes, that's a great idea.   next to the cinema

A Where and when?   near the snack bar

B Let's meet in front of the school   opposite the shop   ...

    at 3 o'clock.   4 o'clock   5:30   4:15   ...

A OK, great. Bye.

B See you later.

Schlage einen anderen Ort oder eine andere Uhrzeit vor.

4 Station 1

12 Your turn: Meeting people
Prepare and make a phone call.
Bereite ein Telefonat vor und führe es durch.

Step 1: Read the dialogue. Use this dialogue as a model.
Lies das Gespräch. Benutze dieses Gespräch als Modell.

Student A
- Hi Emma. Where are you?
- Can we meet later?

- That's boring. What about the park ?
  We can play football there.
- What about four o'clock ?
- Bye.

Student B
- Hi Lena. I'm at home.
- Yes, of course. Let's have a snack at the snack bar .

- That's great. Let's meet at 3:30 .
- Cool. See you later. Bye.

Step 2: Write the activity, the place and the time on a card.
Schreibe die Aktivität, den Ort und die Zeit auf eine Karte.

- What do you want to do?
- Where do you want to meet?
- When do you want to meet?

go swimming
swimming pool
3:30

have a snack   watch a film   …
snack bar   at home
at the cinema   …
five o'clock   seven o'clock   …

Step 3: Use your card to make a phone call. Swap roles.
Nutze deine Karte und spiele ein Telefonat. Tauscht die Rollen.

Step 4: Act a phone call for the class. Spielt euer Telefonat der Klasse vor.

✓ Ich kann ein Treffen vereinbaren.

A tour of Greenwich

1 Listen and put the photos A to D in the right order.
Höre zu und setze die Fotos A bis D in die richtige Reihenfolge.

A

B

C

1

D

2 Listen again. Circle the right word.
Höre nochmal zu. Kreise das richtige Wort ein.

1. There are **three** | **two** museums in the park.
2. The ship is now **a museum** | **a café**.
3. The trip by cable car is **fifteen** | **ten** minutes.
4. You **can** | **can't** have lunch at Greenwich Market.

> Lies dir die Sätze vor dem Hören durch. Dann weißt du, auf was du besonders achten musst.

✓ Ich kann eine Stadtführung verstehen.

4 Station 2

Finding your way

1 Read the dialogue. Lies das Gespräch.

Lena is a tourist from Germany. She's in Greenwich Park and wants to go to the National Maritime Museum. She meets Joshua and Noam.

Lena	Excuse me, can you help me please?
Joshua	Yes, of course.
Lena	Can you tell me the way to the National Maritime Museum please?
Joshua	Yes, of course. **Go straight on.** ⬆ There's a pond.
Lena	OK.
Joshua	After the pond, **turn right** into Park Row. ↱ There's a car park. After the car park, **turn left**. ↰ The National Maritime Museum is **on the left**. OK?
Lena	How long does it take?
Noam	Five minutes.
Lena	Thank you.
Joshua	You're welcome.

2 Look at the maps. Which route is correct? A or B? Tick.
Schaue die Karten an. Welcher Weg ist richtig? A oder B? Setze ein Häkchen.

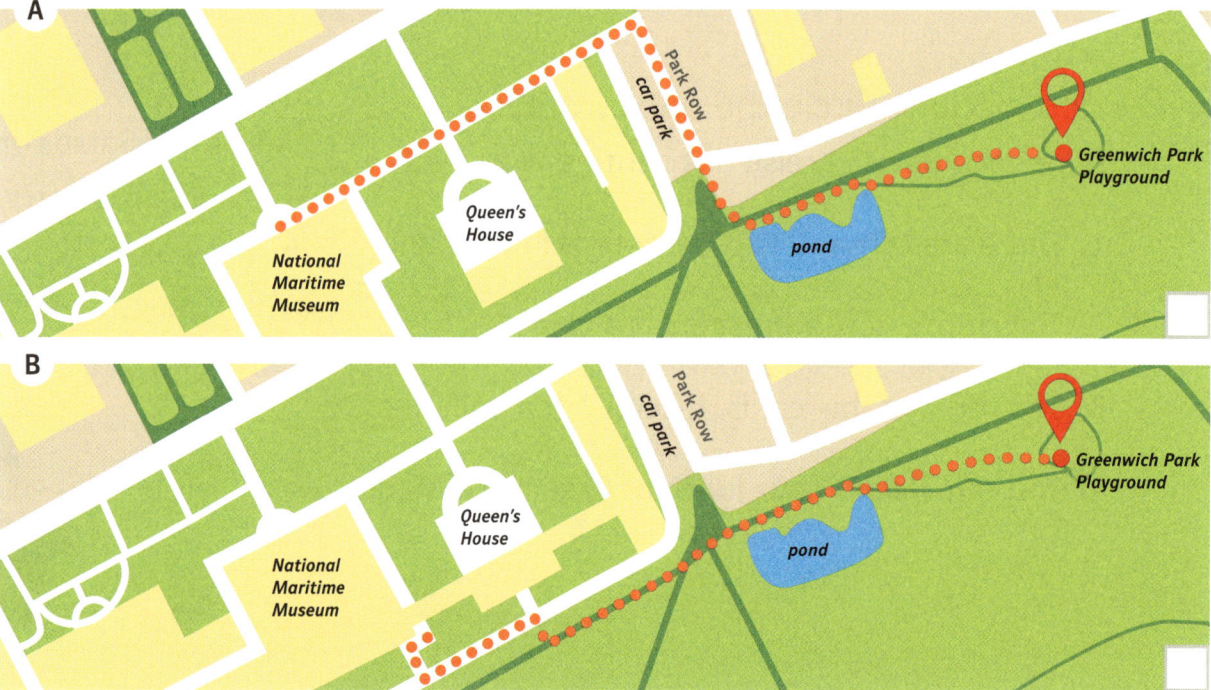

3 Match the sentences with the pictures. ▶ Vokabeln Seite 127 (V16)

Ordne die Sätze den Bildern zu.

1. Go **straight on**. F
2. **Turn** right. ☐
3. **Cross** the road. ☐
4. It's **on the corner**. ☐
5. It's **next to** the shop. ☐
6. It's **opposite** the shop. ☐

A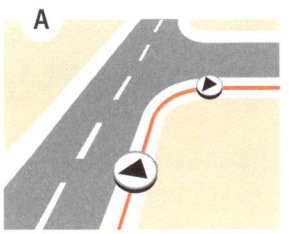
D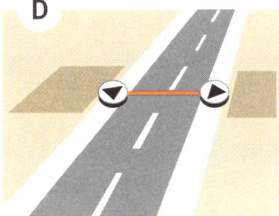
B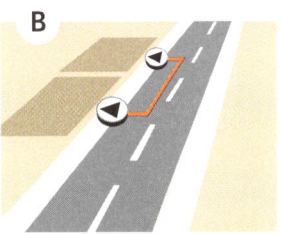
E
C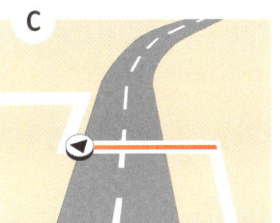
F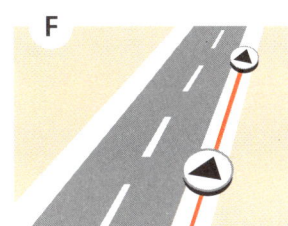

> **Culture**
>
> In England fährt man auf der linken Straßenseite statt der rechten. Wenn man dort über die Straße geht, muss man deshalb zuerst nach rechts und dann nach links schauen.

4 Play the game. Spielt das Spiel.

1. Schüler/in A verlässt den Klassenraum.
2. Die Klasse versteckt einen Gegenstand in der Klasse.
3. Schüler/in A kommt in die Klasse zurück.
4. Schüler/in B beschreibt ihm oder ihr den Weg, um den Gegenstand zu finden.
5. Wechselt euch ab.

Turn left. … Go on. … Stop. That's it.

4 Station 2

5 Mediation

Du bist mit deinen Eltern in der Touristeninformation in Greenwich.
Deine Eltern schauen sich um und bleiben vor diesem Aushang stehen.
Du verstehst am besten Englisch. Beantworte die Fragen deiner Eltern.

Walking tours of Greenwich

Learn all about the history of the city.
Visit the Royal Observatory,
the National Maritime Museum,
Cutty Sark and Greenwich Market

- There are tours every day (11 a.m., 3 p.m.).
- Tours cost £10 for adults and £5 for children.
- Meet in front of the tourist information centre.

1. Wie viele Sehenswürdigkeiten kann man sehen? *vier*
2. Heute ist Montag. Gibt es da auch eine Tour? _____
3. Wie viel kostet eine Tour für uns drei? _____

6 Write the words under the right photos. ► Vokabeln Seite 128 (V17)
Schreibe die Wörter unter die richtigen Fotos.

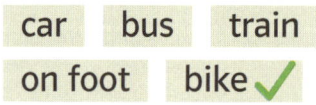
car   bus   train
on foot   bike ✓

C
c_____

D
t_____

A
bike

B
b_____

E
o_____

Station 2 | 4

7 What are the right numbers? Tick.
Wie lauten die richtigen Zahlen?
Setze ein Häkchen.

Bei Busnummern werden die Zahlen manchmal auch einzeln gesprochen: 129 – one, two, nine

1. bus number one hundred and twenty-nine
   - ✓ bus number 129
   - ☐ bus number 134

2. bus number four hundred and eighty-six
   - ☐ bus number 486
   - ☐ bus number 493

3. platform number two
   - ☐ platform number 4
   - ☐ platform number 2

4. twenty minutes
   - ☐ 30 minutes
   - ☐ 20 minutes

5. fifteen minutes
   - ☐ 50 minutes
   - ☐ 15 minutes

6. ten minutes
   - ☐ 10 minutes
   - ☐ 20 minutes

8 Ask your classmates.
Frage deine Mitschülerinnen und Mitschüler.

Auf Englisch sagt man *go **by** car*, *go **by** bike* und *go **by** bus*. Aber es heißt *go **on** foot*.

A How do you go to school?
B I go on foot .
A How long does it take?
B It takes twenty minutes.

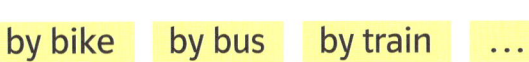

4 Station 2

9 Your turn: Giving directions ▶ Vokabeln Seite 127 (V16)
Give each other directions to places in town. Start at the school.
Gebt einander Wegbeschreibungen zu Orten in der Stadt. Beginnt an der Schule.

Step 1: Look at the map and read the dialogue.
Schau dir die Karte an und lies das Gespräch.

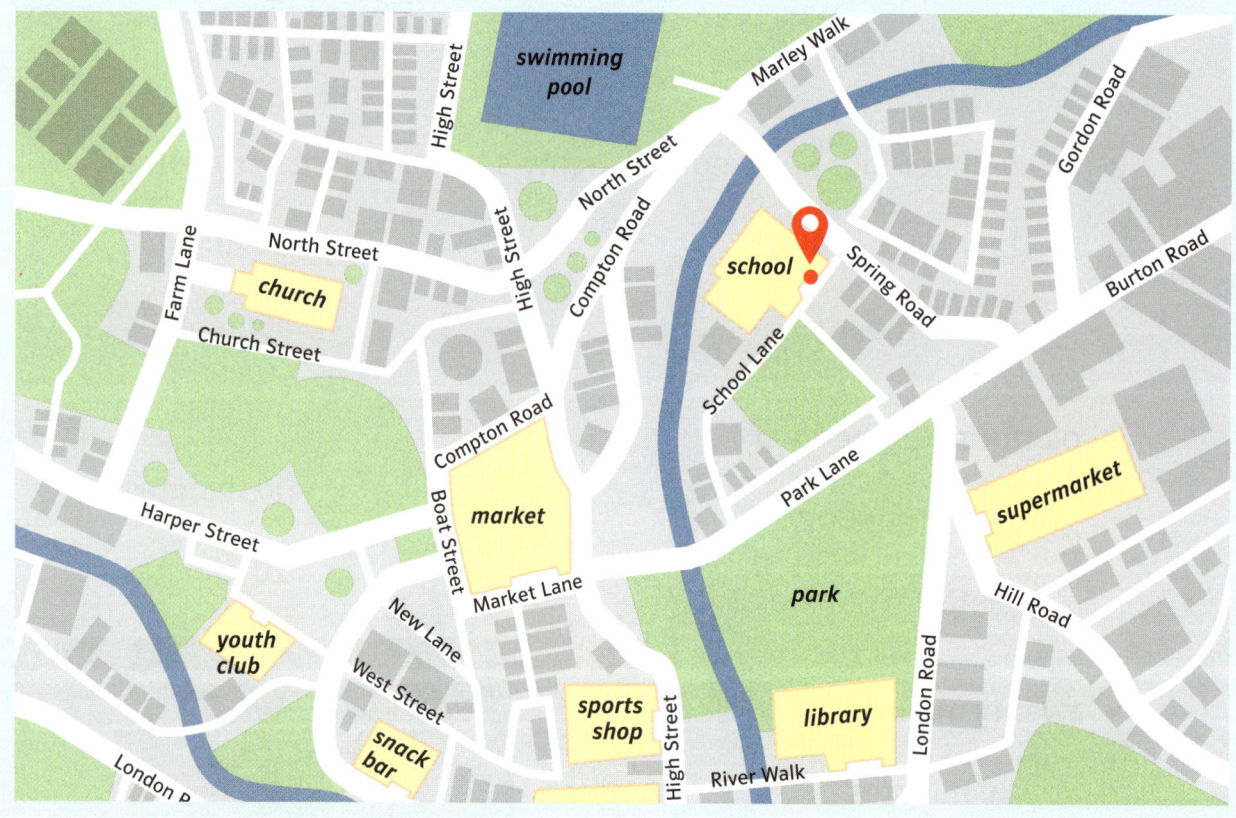

A Can you tell me the way to the sports shop , please?
B Yes, of course. Go straight on . Turn right into Park Lane . Cross the river . Then turn left into High Street . The sports shop is on the right .
A Thank you.
B You're welcome. Bye!

the library | the market | …
turn left | cross the road | …
School Lane | …
on the left | opposite the …
next to the … | …

Step 2: Make your own dialogues. Choose different places.
Führt eure eigenen Gespräche. Wählt andere Orte aus.

✓ Ich kann einen Weg beschreiben.

Viewing 4

Getting around in Greenwich

1 Ask questions and answer them. ▶ Vokabeln Seite 128 (V17)
Stellt die Fragen und beantwortet sie.

1. Can you ride a bike?
2. Do you have a skateboard?
3. Do you like boats?
4. When do you take the train?

2 Watch the film. Which means of transport is <u>not</u> in the film? Tick.
V 9 Schau dir den Film an. Welches Verkehrsmittel kommt nicht im Film vor? Setze ein Häkchen.

A
B
C
D
E
F

3 Draw your dream vehicle. Zeichne dein Traumfahrzeug.

✓ Ich kann eine Doku über Verkehrsmittel verstehen.

4 Reading

A 28

Where is Ruby?

London City News

London City News by Abir Nasser on 9th May

Kangaroo on the run

12:32
London Zoo — There is a hole[1] in the fence[2] of the zoo.
One kangaroo isn't there.
We need your help.

12:52
Geraldo's restaurant — Help! There is a kangaroo in my restaurant. It loves pizza!

13:05
Geraldo's restaurant — The police are at Geraldo's restaurant, but the kangaroo isn't there.

13:42
Shopping centre — We have news from the shopping centre: "There is a kangaroo in the toy shop. It has two toy kangaroos," says Lucy Davies.

14:48
FOOTBALL NEWS — The game is very difficult today.
Oh no, what's that?
There is a kangaroo on the pitch. They must stop the game … Goal! Goal!
The kangaroo is the hero.
Now the police are there.

16:15
London Zoo — Ruby the kangaroo is back at the zoo.
She is OK.
Thank you for your help.

1 hole – *das Loch*; 2 fence – *der Zaun*

Reading 4

1 Read the text. Lies den Text.

2 Match the questions with the correct answers.
Ordne die Fragen den richtigen Antworten zu.

1. Where is Ruby's home? — London Zoo
2. What does she eat at Geraldo's restaurant?
3. When does the police arrive at the restaurant?
4. What does she take from the toy shop?
5. Who is the hero at the football game?

two toy kangaroos

13:05

London Zoo

Ruby

pizza

3 Put the sentences in the right order and write them down.
Setze die Sätze in die richtige Reihenfolge und schreibe sie auf.

The kangaroo is at a football game. ☐

A kangaroo goes into a restaurant. ☐

London Zoo needs help. *1*

The kangaroo is in a toy shop. ☐

The kangaroo is back at the zoo. ☐

The police arrive on the football pitch. ☐

1. *London Zoo needs help.*
2.
3.
4.
5.
6.

✓ Ich kann einen Newsticker verstehen.

4 Check out

Task: An audio guide

Make an audio guide about famous places in your town.
Erstellt einen Audioguide über berühmte Orte in deiner Stadt.

Step 1: Which are your favourite places?
Was sind eure Lieblingsorte?
1. Macht eine Liste in der Klasse.
2. Bildet zu viert Gruppen.
3. Jede Gruppe wählt einen anderen Ort.

> snack bar
> cinema
> shopping centre
> ...

Step 2: What's interesting about your place?
Was ist an eurem Ort so interessant?
1. Sammelt Ideen. Zeichnet eine Mindmap.
2. Schreibt den Text.

> meet friends
> youth club
> every day

David	Hello. Welcome to the Kranichstein audio guide. We are Zelal, Mona, Osman and David.
Zelal	Do you want to meet friends and play games? You can go to the Kranichstein youth club every day.
Mona	The youth club is open from 3:00 to 6:00.
Osman	You can find us in Hauptstraße 50, opposite the school. See you there.

Step 3: Check and practise. Prüfe und übe.
1. Prüf deinen Text. Bitte einen Lehrer oder eine Lehrerin um Hilfe.
2. Übe die schwierigen Wörter.
3. Lies den Text deiner Gruppe vor.

Step 4: Record and check. Nimm auf und prüfe.
Nimm deinen Text auf. Dann höre ihn dir an. Kannst du alles verstehen? Wenn nicht, nimm ihn nochmal auf.

Step 5: Present your audio guide in class.
Stelle deinen Audioguide der Klasse vor.

4 Discover

A walk around town

Which photos are from England? Which are from Germany?
Use the clues in the photos.

Welche Fotos sind aus England? Welche sind aus Deutschland?
Achtet auf die Hinweise auf den Fotos.

England

1, _____

Germany

6, _____

5 Around the year

Am Ende dieser Unit kann ich …
- über Jahreszeiten sprechen.
- über das vergangene Jahr sprechen.
- eine Reportage verstehen.
- einen Tagebucheintrag schreiben.
- Interviews verstehen.
- eine Legende verstehen.

My favourite **season** is **spring**.
I can meet my friends outside.

I like **summer**. It's **hot** and **sunny**.
We can go to the swimming pool.

Autumn is OK.
The trees are beautiful.

I don't like **winter**.
It's often **cold**.

Check in 5

1 Write the words in the right group. ▶ Vokabeln Seite 129 (V18)
Jahreszeiten: Schreibe die Wörter in die richtige Gruppe.

cold   beautiful trees   hot and sunny   go to the swimming pool

meet friends outside ✓

🌷 spring: *meet friends outside*

☀️ summer:

🍂 autumn:

❄️ winter:

2 **Your turn: My seasons**

a) Say what you like or don't like about two seasons.
Sagt über zwei Jahreszeiten, was ihr mögt oder nicht mögt.

My favourite season is winter .   spring   summer   autumn

I often go ice skating .   play games   watch a film

I don't like autumn .   do sport   go cycling   …

I can't play outside .

It's often cold .   hot   sunny

b) Draw a picture of your favourite season.
Male ein Bild von deiner Lieblingsjahreszeit.

✓ Ich kann über Jahreszeiten sprechen.

Elliot's year

1 Read the text about Elliot's year. Lies den Text über Elliots Jahr.

1st January:
The fireworks on New Year **were** beautiful.

23rd March:
My birthday present **was** a cool bike!

6th April:
We **had** a cake sale at school.

10th June:
I **was** nervous about the exams.

August:
I **spent** the summer holidays in Cornwall. It often **rained**.

15th December:
Mum and I **went** to a Christmas market.

2 Match the events with the right months.
Ordne die Ereignisse den richtigen Monaten zu.

cake sale   Christmas market   fireworks ✓   Elliot's birthday   exams

summer holidays

1. January: *fireworks*
2. March: _____
3. April: _____
4. June: _____
5. August: _____
6. December: _____

3 Write down the months Elliot didn't talk about. ▶ Vokabeln Seite 129 (V18)
Schreibe die Monate auf, über die Elliot nicht sprach.

February ✓   May   July   September   October   November

January   *February*   March   April   June

August   December

4 Numbers and Dates. Zahlen und Datumsangaben. ▶ Vokabeln Seite 118 (V4)

a) Match the numbers with the words. Verbinde die Zahlen mit den Wörtern.

1st   2nd   3rd   4th   12th   20th   35th

second   twentieth   first   third   thirty-fifth   fourth   twelfth

b) How do you write the dates Elliot talked about?
Wie schreibt man die Datumsangaben, über die Elliot spricht?

1st January: *the first of January*

23rd March: _____

6th April: _____

10th June: _____

15th December: _____

> **Culture**
> In England **schreibt** man das Datum so: *9th March 2025*
> Man **sagt** das Datum so:
> *the ninth of March twenty twenty-five*

5 Ask a partner about his or her birthday.
Frage einen Partner oder eine Partnerin nach deren Geburtstag.

A When is your birthday?   B My birthday is the 25th of July.

> **Language**
> Ein Verb mit **ed** am Ende bedeutet, dass etwas in der Vergangenheit geschehen ist.
>
> We play**ed** games. Wir spielten Spiele.

6 Complete the sentences about last Saturday.
Vervollständige die Sätze über letzten Samstag.

called   helped   watched ✓   played

1. Elliot _watched_ a film at the cinema. (schaute sich an)
2. Joshua _____ football in the park. (spielte)
3. Katie _____ Kira with her homework. (half)
4. Nisha _____ her aunt. (rief an)

7 Match the right sentence parts. Verbinde die richtigen Satzteile.

Rocky turned — in front of Joshua's home.
He crossed the road — with Joshua.
Joshua watched — into Roan Street.
He called — "Rocky, where were you?"
Rocky stayed — his grandpa Osaro.
Later Grandpa Osaro — Rocky from the door.
He asked: — arrived.

8 Match the right words. Use the right colour.
Ordne die Wörter richtig zu. Verwende die richtige Farbe.

Manche Wörter sehen in der Vergangenheit ganz anders aus. Die deutschen Wörter helfen dir bei der Zuordnung!

we go	we have	we do	we see	it is	we are
wir gehen	wir haben	wir machen	wir sehen	es ist	wir sind

we had	we saw	we went	we were	we did	it was
wir hatten	wir sahen	wir gingen	wir waren	wir machten	es war

9 Complete Elliot's postcard. Use the words from exercise 8.
Fülle Elliots Postkarte aus. Benutze die Wörter aus Übung 8.

Hi Harry,

Cornwall is cool. We *went* swimming on Monday

and we _____ fish for lunch. (gingen, hatten)

We _____ a lot of nice things. (machten)

On Tuesday we _____ at the museum

in Charlestown. (waren) We _____ a lot of cool old ships. (sahen)

It _____ great. (war)

Bye, Elliot

10 Talk about your weekend.
Sprecht über euer Wochenende.

On Saturday I was at a party . watched a film played games

On Sunday … slept a lot. …

5 Station 1

11 Your turn: My special day
Talk about last year. Prepare a presentation with a poster.
Sprich über das letzte Jahr. Bereite eine Präsentation mit einem Poster vor.

Step 1: Choose a photo of a special day from last year.
Such dir ein Foto von einem besonderen Tag des letzten Jahres aus.

Media tip
Wenn Personen auf deinem Foto sind, musst du sie vorher fragen. Du kannst auch nur einen Ausschnitt oder einen Gegenstand zeigen.

Step 2: Write a text.
Schreibe einen Text.

Hier ist ein Mustertext für dich.

My special day

This picture was in `summer` .   `spring` `autumn` `winter`

`My birthday` was great.   `The party` `The trip` `…`

We were `at home` .   `at the sea` `in … (Name des Ortes)`

You can see `me` here.   `my mum` `my dog` `my cake`

It was `cool` .   `funny` `nice`

Step 3: Make a poster
Mache ein Poster.

My birthday (15th August)

Step 4: Practise your text.
Übe deinen Text.

Skills
Lies langsam und deutlich. Mache nach jedem Satz eine kleine Pause.

Step 5: Present your poster.
Präsentiere dein Poster.

✓ Ich kann über das vergangene Jahr sprechen.

Viewing 5

Pancake time!

1 Do you like pancakes? Tick what you eat them with.
Magst du Pfannkuchen? Sätze Häkchen, womit du sie isst.

pancake   sugar   chocolate   jam

I like pancakes. ☐	I don't like pancakes. ☐
I often have them with sugar. ☐	I don't have them with sugar. ☐
I often have them with chocolate. ☐	I don't have them with chocolate. ☐
I often have them with jam. ☐	I don't have them with jam. ☐

2 Watch the film. Put the headings in the right order.
V 11
Schaue dir den Film an. Setze die Überschriften in die richtige Reihenfolge.

A A special day ☐
B Pancakes and you ☐
C How to make a pancake **1**
D Pancake races ☐
E What to eat with a pancake ☐

3 Make your own pancakes. Ask your teacher for the recipe.
Backe deine eigenen Pfannkuchen. Frage deinen Lehrer oder deine Lehrerin nach dem Rezept.

✓ Ich kann eine Reportage verstehen.

5 Station 2

Sunny days and rainy days

1 Read the text. Lies den Text. ▶ Vokabeln Seite 130 (V19)

Katie Yesterday Kira and I went to Brighton with our dad.
It was **warm** and **sunny** there.
We went to the beach.
But the water was **cold**.
Later we had ice creams and
I went on the roller coaster.

Nisha I went there two years ago.
It was great.

Katie Yes, we loved it too.

2 What can you see in the pictures? Write the words.
Was kannst du auf den Bildern sehen? Schreibe die Wörter auf.

Katie   Kira   dad   beach   water ✓   ice creams   roller coaster

water

3 Listen and say

a) Listen and say the words.
Hör zu und sprich die Wörter nach.
A 29

weather   was   warm

very   November

b) Listen and say the sentence.
Hör zu und sprich den Satz nach.
A 30

The weather was very warm.

90

4 What a day! ▶ Vokabeln Seite 130 (V19)

a) Match each box with the right picture.
Verbinde jeden Kasten mit dem richtigen Bild.

| sun   sunny   hot ✓ | snow   cold | cloud   cloudy   warm | rain   rainy   wind   windy |

b) Write the right description under each picture.
Schreibe die richtige Beschreibung unter jedes Bild.

no rain   a lot of sun   snow ✓   cloud   no wind   a lot of rain

A: snow

5 Talk about the weather in your town.
Sprich über das Wetter in deiner Stadt.

Today it's *sunny*. There is no *rain*.   cold   windy   hot

Yesterday it was *cloudy*. There was no *snow*.   sun   wind   cloud

5 Station 2

> **Language**
> Wenn in einem Satz **didn't** steht, ist etwas in der Vergangenheit **nicht** geschehen oder jemand hat etwas **nicht** gemacht.
>
> We **didn't win**. Wir gewannen nicht.

6 Write the matching sentence under each photo.
Schreibe den passenden Satz unter jedes Foto.

| It didn't rain in Brighton. | Katie's dad didn't have an ice cream |

| Kira didn't go on the roller coaster. ✓ |

A    B    C

Kira didn't go

on the roller coaster.

7 What didn't you do on Saturday? Write three sentences.
Was hast du am Samstag nicht gemacht? Schreibe drei Sätze.

On Saturday I didn't + do my homework.
help my grandma.
buy new pens.

1. *On Saturday I didn't do*
2.
3.

Station 2 5

> **Language**
> Wenn am Ende eines Wortes **n't** steht, bedeutet das immer **not** (auf Deutsch: nicht).
>
> I **wasn't** happy. Ich **war nicht** glücklich.
> They **weren't** there. Sie **waren nicht** da.

8 Katie's bad day

a) Match the sentence parts.
Verbinde die Satzteile.

1. Friday wasn't   E at home. He was outside.
2. I wasn't   A happy.
3. The weather wasn't   I at home. They were at the zoo.
4. My mum and Kira weren't   K a good day.
5. Milo wasn't   T nice.

b) Put the letters on the right in the right order. What's the word?
Setze die Buchstaben rechts in die richtige Reihenfolge. Wie heißt das Wort?

| K | | | | |

9 Mediation

Ein Freund möchte einer englischen Klasse im Videochat von seinem letzten Ausflug berichten, weiß aber nicht alle Wörter. Hilf ihm, den Text zu schreiben.

didn't take   fairground ✓   were fun   very big   people

1. My family and I went to the _fairground_ in town. (Rummel)
2. It's near the river and there are _____ fish for lunch. (riesig)
3. We _____ our dog because there were

   too many _____ . (nahmen nicht mit, Leute)
4. The roller coasters _____ . (machten Spaß)

5 Station 2

10 Your turn: A diary entry
Make a diary entry about last Saturday or Sunday.
Gestalte einen Tagebucheintrag über letzten Samstag oder Sonntag.

Step 1: Collect ideas about last weekend.
Sammle Ideen vom letzten Wochenende.

Sunday, 15th June

I played with my friends .   saw grandma / grandpa   watched a film

We had a lot of fun.   went to … (Ort) with my family   …

But it was hot .   the weather was bad   it was rainy   …

Later we had ice creams .   my favourite cake   pizza   …

That was cool .   great   nice   funny   …

Step 2: Make a draft. Start with the date. Write sentences.
Schreibe einen Entwurf. Beginne mit dem Datum. Schreibe Sätze.

Step 3: Write and design your diary entry.
Schreibe und gestalte deinen Tagebucheintrag.

- Choose a nice piece of paper.   Wähle ein schönes Papier aus.
- Add a photo or draw a picture.   Füge ein Foto hinzu oder male ein Bild.

✓ Ich kann einen Tagebucheintrag schreiben.

A day to remember

Skills
Bilder helfen dir, einen Hörtext zu verstehen.

1 Match the words with the pictures.
Ordne die Wörter den Bildern zu.

a garden ✓   a camp ✓   a dog   night   rainy   sunny

a garden, _____   a camp, _____

2 Listen to the interview. Which picture from exercise 1 is it about?
Höre dir das Interview an. Um welches Interview aus Aufgabe 1 geht es?

A ☐   B ☐

3 Text messages ▶ Vokabeln Seite 130 (V19)

a) Read the text message. Write the words for the emojis.
Lies die Nachricht. Schreibe die Wörter für die Emojis auf.

tent   bad   wind   rain   bad   car

What a 😭 trip! The weather was 😭 too. There was a lot of ☔ and 💨.
We didn't sleep in the ⛺. We stayed in the 🚗.

b) Write a text message like in a). Use pictures.
Can your partner read the text?
Schreibe einen Text wie in a). Benutze Bilder. Kann dein Partner oder deine Partnerin den Text lesen?

✓ Ich kann Interviews verstehen.

5 Reading

My first day with Robin Hood

A 32

Culture

Robin Hood war ein Volksheld. Er lebte im Mittelalter im Sherwood Forest, einem großen Wald in Mittelengland. Er stahl von den Reichen Geld und gab es den Armen. Sein größter Feind war der Sheriff von Nottingham.

It was my first day with Robin Hood in the forest. I was twelve and so excited. "Listen," Robin said. "The sheriff's men have a girl at their camp. She took some apples. But the apples are for everyone. We must free the girl." Robin looked at me. "Peter, you can help us." I was proud. We stopped near the camp of the sheriff's men.
"There are eight men with swords," he said. "The girl is in a tent. Peter, can you crawl[1] under the tent and free the girl?"
"Yes, of course," I said. Then Robin fired[2] an arrow into the sheriff's hat. The sheriff's men were surprised and didn't know what to do.

I crawled under the tent and freed the girl. Then we took the horses and rode into the forest.
"I'm Matilda. Who are you?" asked the girl.
"I'm Peter, one of Robin Hood's men. You are very good with horses," I said.
"Thank you. Can I come with you?" she said.
"Great idea!" Robin said behind us.

1 to crawl – *kriechen*; 2 to fire – *abfeuern; schießen*

Reading 5

1 What do you know about Robin Hood? Tick the right answer.
Was weißt du über Robin Hood? Setze ein Häkchen bei der richtigen Antwort.

1. Robin Hood was a ☐ hero. ☐ bad man. ☐ funny man.

2. He lived in ☐ England. ☐ a castle. ☐ a village.

3. He always helped ☐ horses. ☐ the sheriff. ☐ people.

2 Match the words with the right person. Colour them in the right person's colour.
Ordne die Wörter den richtigen Personen zu. Male sie in der Farbe der richtigen Person aus.

Peter   Matilda   Robin

twelve   helps people   is in a tent

good with arrows   small   took apples

3 Complete the crossword. Vervollständige das Kreuzworträtsel.

apples   hat   tent   forest   horse   arrows ✓

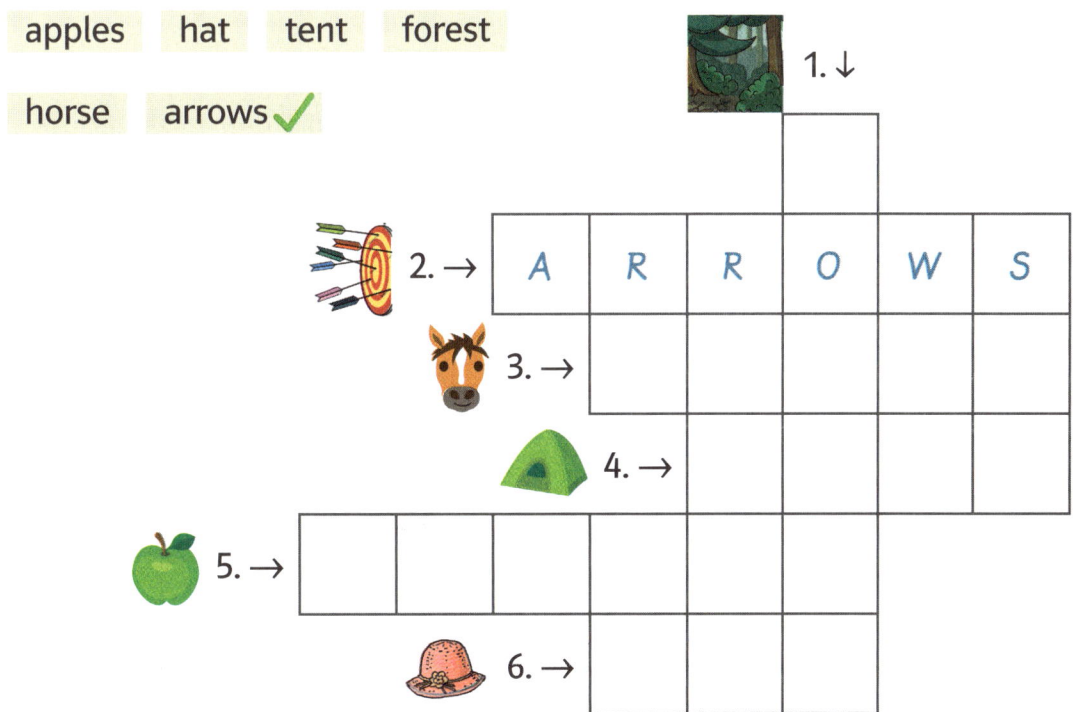

✓ Ich kann eine Legende verstehen.

5 Check out

Task: A yearbook

Make a yearbook for your class. Write it on paper or use a computer.
Erstellt ein Jahrbuch für eure Klasse. Erstellt es auf Papier oder am Computer.

Step 1: Get into groups.
Teilt euch in Gruppen auf.

A: spring   (March – May)
B: summer (June – August)
C: autumn   (September – November)
D: winter   (December – February)

Step 2: Make notes about one yearbook entry for your season.
Macht euch Notizen zu einem Jahrbucheintrag für eure Jahreszeit.
– Was habt ihr erlebt?
– Wo wart ihr?
– Wer war dabei?
– Wie war es?

party   cake sale   class trip

classroom   playground   …

classmates   teacher   parents

great   cool   nice   …

Step 3: Write the text. Find photos or draw pictures.
Schreibt den Text. Findet Fotos oder malt Bilder.
– Wer schreibt den Text?
– Wer macht das Layout?
– Wer überprüft den Text?

June: **SCHOOL PARTY**
We had a big party in the playground. Our classmates, our teachers and parents were there. It was a great day!

Step 4: Bring all four seasons together to make the yearbook.
Tragt alle vier Jahreszeiten zusammen und erstellt das Jahrbuch.

Let's celebrate!

Viele Menschen, deren Eltern oder Großeltern aus anderen Ländern nach England kamen, brachten ihre Festtage und Traditionen mit. Heute sind diese Festtage Teil des englischen Lebens.

1 Christmas Day, 25th December
People open their Christmas presents on this day.
There is a big family meal.

2 Diwali, in October or November
There are special lights and presents for family and friends.

3 Easter, in March or April
People go to church.
Then they eat Easter eggs.

4 Halloween, 31st October
There are cool parties.
Kids have costumes and go 'trick or treating'.

1 Which special days do you know? Tick your answers.
Welche Feiertage kennst du? Setze Häkchen.

I know ☐ Christmas. ☐ Diwali. ☐ Easter. ☐ Halloween.

2 Talk about festivals in your family.
Sprecht über Feste in eurer Familie.

We celebrate Christmas .   Eid   Easter   Halloween   …

We have a big meal .   a party   special lights   costumes

We get presents too.   eat Easter eggs   have cakes   …

6 Out and about

Am Ende dieser Unit kann ich …
- Ausflugsziele benennen.
- mich über Ausflüge unterhalten.
- ein Hörspiel verstehen.
- Essen und Trinken bestellen.
- eine Videoanleitung zu Rezepten verstehen.
- Infotexte verstehen.

A

B

There are some cool places near Greenwich. I sometimes go to the **swimming pool** in my holidays.

C

There's a great **skate park** near Greenwich too. It's free.

D

Our class went on a **school trip** last year. We visited a **farm**.

E
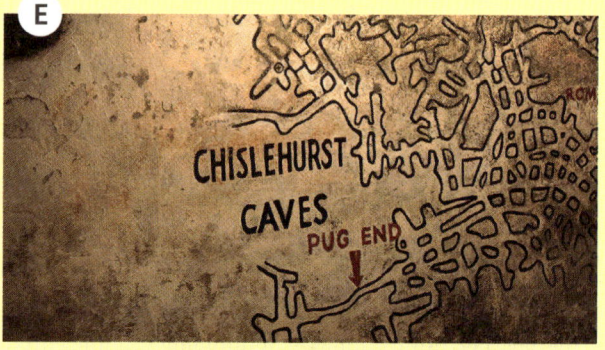

There are some **scary caves** in London. You can go there by train.

Check in 6

1 Places to visit

a) Match the captions with the photos.
Ordne die Überschriften den Fotos zu.

1. Free fun! — That's picture C.
2. Sport is great! — That's picture ____.
3. A scary place! — That's picture ____.
4. A cool place for a hot summer day! — That's picture ____.
5. Come and see our farm animals! — That's picture ____.

b) Write the words under the right pictures.
Schreibe die Wörter unter die richtigen Bilder.

cave   free   farm   scary

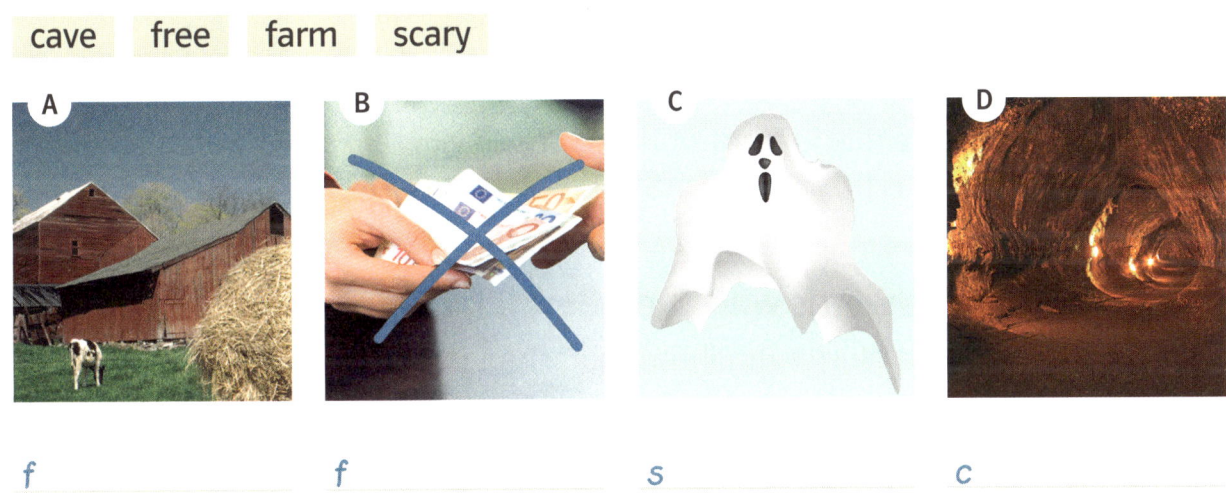

A f ____   B f ____   C s ____   D c ____

2 Your turn: Write about a place in or near your town.
Schreibe über einen Ort in oder in der Nähe deines Wohnorts.

There's a nice in lake in my town.   castle   park   cave   …   near

I was there at the weekend.   yesterday   last summer   …

You can go swimming there.   play games   do sport   …

I like it because it's fun.   beautiful   interesting   nice   …

✓ Ich kann Ausflugsziele benennen.

6 Station 1

Activities week

1 Read the text. Lies den Text.

This week there's an activities week for Year 7. Joshua and Nisha meet in the afternoon.

Joshua What **did you do** on the first day?
Nisha I **visited** the organic farm. It was cool. We **collected** eggs and **milked** a cow.
Joshua **Did** you drink the milk?
Nisha No, I **didn't**. But I **made** my own yoghurt. How **was** your day?
Joshua Great. I **went** climbing at the climbing wall.
Nisha **Was** it dangerous?
Joshua No, it **wasn't**. I think Harry **wasn't** happy.
Nisha Why?
Joshua The people in front of him **were** so slow.
Nisha Oh no!

2 Match these words with their German meaning.
Verbinde diese Wörter mit ihrer deutschen Bedeutung.

1. visit   die Kuh
2. organic   gefährlich
3. collect eggs   besuchen
4. cow   das Klettern
5. yoghurt   Bio-
6. climbing   langsam
7. dangerous   Eier sammeln
8. slow   der Joghurt

3 What did the students do yesterday? Tick.

Was haben die Schülerinnen und Schüler gestern gemacht? Setze Häkchen.

1. Nisha drank cow milk. ☐ made yoghurt. ☐
2. Joshua's day at the climbing wall was great. ☐ wasn't great. ☐
3. Harry was slow. ☐ wasn't happy. ☐

4 How was it?

a) Match these words with their opposites. Use the right colour.

Ordne diese Wörter ihren Gegenteilen zu. Verwende die richtige Farbe.

easy   good   fast   interesting   safe

bad   boring   dangerous   difficult   slow

b) Find the opposites, circle them and write them down.

Finde die Gegenteile, kreise sie ein und schreibe sie auf.

A	D	I	F	F	I	C	U	L	T
H	I	B	A	D	R	E	T	Z	O
S	L	O	W	A	G	S	V	E	L
I	D	A	N	G	E	R	O	U	S

easy ↔ *difficult*
good ↔ ___
fast ↔ ___
safe ↔ ___

5 Listen and say.

a) Listen and say the words. Höre zu und sprich die Wörter nach.

A 33

[aʊ] h**ow** | n**ow** | br**ow**n | c**ow** | m**ou**ntain
[əʊ] g**o** | sl**ow** | kn**ow** | s**o**

b) Listen and say the sentences.

A 34

Höre zu und sage die Sätze.

How does the brown cow go down
the mountain? It's so slow now.

6 Station 1

Language

So stellst du Fragen über vergangene Aktivitäten:

Did **you** **like** the farm? – Yes, I did. / No I didn't.
Hat dir der Bauernhof gefallen? – Ja. / Nein.

Did **your friends** **go** to the cinema yesterday?
– Yes, they did. / No they didn't.
Sind deine Freunde gestern ins Kino gegangen?
– Ja. / Nein.

Did you eat too many apples again?

6 Make questions and ask them. Swap roles.
Bildet Fragen und stellt sie einander. Tauscht die Rollen.

your parents

meet friends | read a book

A Did **you** visit your grandparents last week ? go climbing | ...

B Yes, **I** did. / No, **I** didn't. on Saturday? | yesterday?

at the weekend? | ...

they

Auch hier gilt wieder: Das Fragewort steht am Anfang.

7 Answer the questions. Beantworte die Fragen.

He went to the climbing wall.   They made yoghurt.

Some people were too slow   She went to the organic farm. ✓

1. Where did Nisha go on Monday?   *She went to the organic farm.*

2. What did the students make there? _____

3. Where did Joshua go on Monday? _____

4. Why did Harry not like it there? _____

Language

So fragst du mit **was** (Einzahl) und **were** (*you* und Mehrzahl) in der Vergangenheit:

Were you at home? – Yes, **I was**. / No, **I wasn't**.
Warst du zu Hause? – Ja. / Nein.

Was it late? – Yes, **it was**. / No, **it wasn't**.
War es spät? – Ja. / Nein.

Were they at school? – Yes, **they were**. / No, **they weren't**.
Waren sie in der Schule? – Ja. / Nein.

8 Complete the answers.
Vervollständige die Antworten.

was ✓   were   was

wasn't   weren't   wasn't

Antworte bei Kurzantworten immer mit dem Wort, mit dem die Frage beginnt.

1. Was Nisha at the organic farm?   Yes, she *was*   .
2. Was the farm interesting?   Yes, it _____   .
3. Was Katie at the farm?   No, she _____   .
4. Were Joshua and Elliot at the climbing wall?   Yes, they _____   .
5. Were Nisha and Harry in one group?   No, they _____   .

9 Ask questions about the picture. Stelle Fragen zum Bild.

Were   Was ✓   Was

1. *Was* _____ Nisha at the park?
2. _____ her parents there too?
3. _____ their neighbours' dog in the park?

10 Your turn: My day trip
Talk about a day trip with the help of a photo.
Sprich mit Hilfe eines Fotos über einen Tagesausflug.

Step 1: Bring your own photo of a day trip. Make notes.
Bringe ein eigenes Foto von einem Tagesausflug mit. Mach dir Notizen.

Where? (Wo?) a castle | the beach | the river | …

When? (Wann?) last weekend | on Saturday | last summer | …

Who? (Wer?) my family | my friends | my grandparents | …

What? (Was?) went on a boat tour | went swimming | visited a museum | …

How? great | interesting | cool | …

Step 2: Ask your partner about the trip. Swap roles.
Frage deine Partnerin oder deinen Partner nach dem Ausflug. Tauscht die Rollen.

Student A	Student B
Hi …, **where** did you go on your trip?	I went to a lake.
When did you go there?	Last Sunday.
Who was with you?	My parents and my brother.
What did you do?	We went kayaking.
How was it?	It was great. How was your trip?

✓ Ich kann mich über Ausflüge unterhalten.

Adventure in the caves

1 Complete the descriptions of the photos.
Vervollständige die Beschreibungen der Bilder.

gold   scary   criminal   angry

1. a s_____ cave
2. jewellery and _____
3. an _____ man
4. a _____

2 Listen and look at the pictures A to F.
Höre zu und schau dir die Bilder A bis F an.

Welcome!

3 Listen again. Write the sentences under the right pictures.
Höre nochmal zu. Schreibe die Sätze unter die richtigen Bilder.

Run!   We don't go there.   Let's go back.   Welcome! ✓

You were great.   Call the police!

✓ Ich kann ein Hörspiel verstehen.

6 Station 2

What would you like to eat?

1 Read the text. Lies den Text.

Joshua and Elliot are at a snack bar.

Assistant	Hello. How can I help you?
Joshua	Hi. I'd like a **cheese** and **tomato sandwich** and a **packet of crisps,** please.
Assistant	Of course. What would you like to drink?
Joshua	A **bottle of lemonade**, please.
Assistant	Would you like an **apple** or a **bar of chocolate**?
Joshua	Can I have a **banana**, please?
Assistant	Here you are. Anything else?
Joshua	No, thank you. How much is it?
Assistant	That's **£4.40**.
Joshua	Here you are.
Assistant	Thank you. Here's your change.
Joshua	Thank you.
Assistant	You're welcome. Bye!

Culture

Eine kleine Packung Chips *(crisps)* gehört in England zu einem Essen oft dazu.

Man schreibt: £4.40
Man sagt: four pounds forty

2 What does Joshua buy? Choose the right receipt.
Was kauft Joshua? Wähle den richtigen Kassenzettel aus.

A
```
      RECEIPT
sandwich 1x    £2.20
  tomato, cucumber
apple 1x       £0.60
orange juice 1x £0.90
crisps 1x      £0.70


   THANK YOU!
```

B
```
      RECEIPT
sandwich 1x    £2.20
  cheese, tomato
crisps 1x      £0.70
lemonade 1x    £0.90
banana 1x      £0.60


   THANK YOU!
```

Station 2 6

3 Write the right words for the food. ▶ Vokabeln Seite 131 (V20)
Schreibe die richtigen Wörter für das Essen.

crisps   chocolate   salad   lemonade   tomato   sandwich ✓

packet   cheese

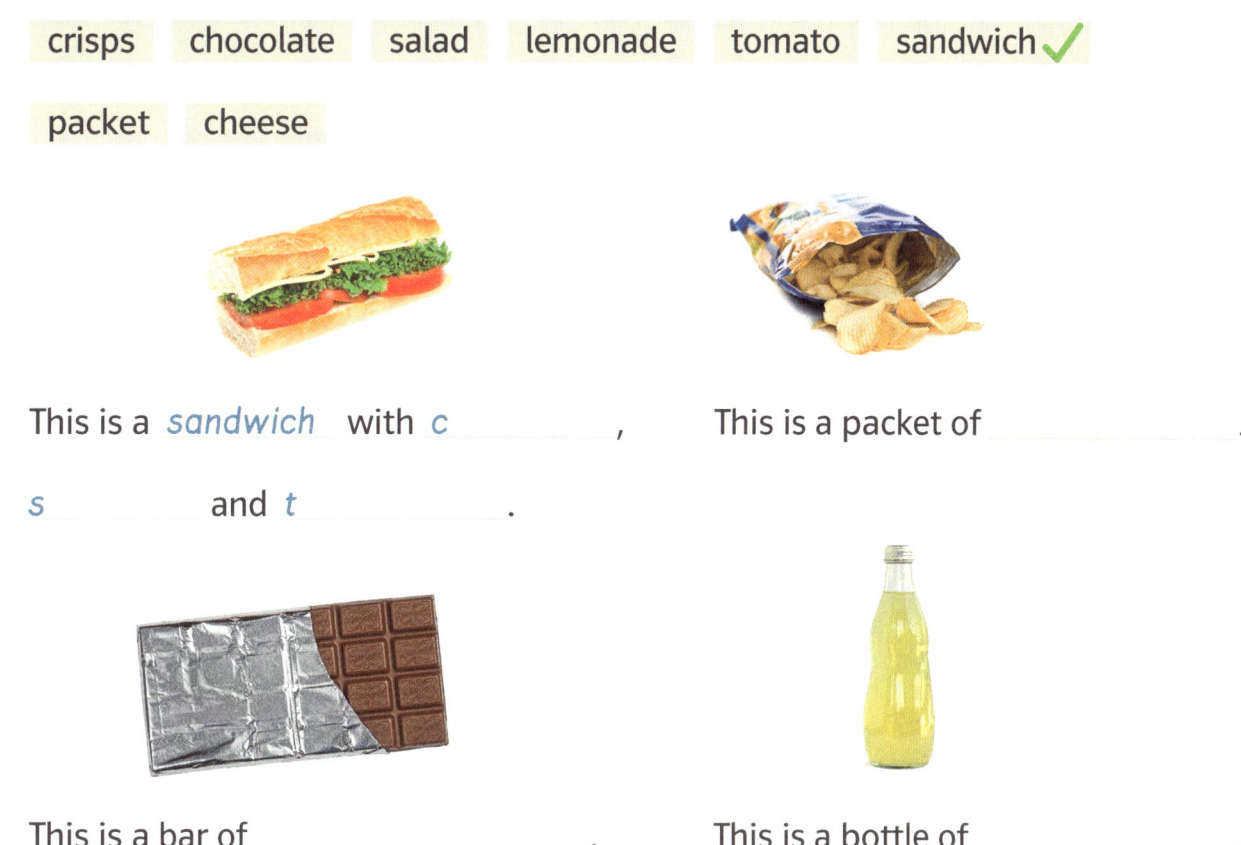

This is a _sandwich_ with c_____,   This is a packet of _____.

s_____ and t_____.

This is a bar of _____.   This is a bottle of _____.

4 Choose the right words for the photos. ▶ Vokabeln Seite 131 (V20)
Wähle die richtigen Wörter für die Fotos aus.

A
milk ☐
cola ☐

B
salad ☐
crisps ☐

C
ham ☐
cheese ☐

D
pasta ☐
eggs ☐

E
cucumber ☐
chips ☐

F
cake ☐
jam ☐

109

6 Station 2

5 Bottles, packets, ... ▶ Vokabeln Seite 132 (V21)

a) Read Katie's notes for the party. What food is in the picture? Circle it.
Lies Katies Notizen für die Party. Welche Lebensmittel sind auf dem Bild zu sehen? Kreise sie ein.

For the party:
- 6 bottles of water
- 4 bottles of orange juice
- 1 bar of white chocolate
- 9 packets of crisps

b) Compare the picture with Katie's notes. Then write the shopping list.
Vergleiche das Bild mit Katies Notizen. Schreibe danach die Einkaufsliste.

in the Bell's kitchen	Katie's shopping list
0 bars of white chocolate	1 bar of white chocolate

🔊 6 Listen to two dialogues. Tick the right answers.
A 36
Höre dir zwei Gespräche an. Setze ein Häkchen bei den richtigen Antworten.

	What did they buy?				How much was it?			
1. Elliot	six eggs	☐	banana joghurt	☐	£1.40	☐	£1.50	☐
2. Nisha	orange juice	☐	apple juice	☐	£1.75	☐	£2.00	☐

110

7 Match the shopping phrases with their German meaning.
Verbinde die Einkaufs-Ausdrücke mit ihrer deutschen Bedeutung.

1. How can I help you?   Hier ist dein / Ihr Wechselgeld.
2. Can I have …, please?   Wie kann ich dir / Ihnen helfen?
3. Anything else?   Kann ich bitte …haben?
4. How much is it?   Noch etwas?
5. That's £5.50.   Gern geschehen. Tschüss.
6. Here's your change.   Das macht £5.50.
7. You're welcome. Bye.   Wie viel kostet es?

8 Make shopping dialogues. You can use the phrases from exercise 7.
Führt Einkaufsgespräche. Ihr könnt die Ausdrücke aus Aufgabe 7 benutzen.

A Hello, how can I help you?
B Hello. Can I have two bottles of water , please?
A Of course. Anything else?
B Yes, please. A bar of chocolate , please. How much is it?
A That's £2.80 .
B Here you are.
A Thank you. Here's your change.
B Thank you. Bye.
A You're welcome. Bye.

6 Station 2

9 Your turn: At a snack bar ▶ Vokabeln Seite 131 und 132 (V20–21)
Practice different dialogues. Übt verschiedene Gespräche.

Step 1: Read the menu. Lest die Speisekarte.

MENU

Sandwiches
- Ham £2.10
- Cheese £1.90
- Ham & cheese £2.70
- Cheese & tomato ... £2.20
- Tomato & salad £1.60
- Egg £2.30

Drinks
- Water £0.90
- Lemonade £1.10
- Milk £0.90
- Juice
  - Orange £0.80
  - Apple £0.80
  - Tomato £0.80

Snacks
- Crisps £0.90
- Chocolate £0.70
- Cake £1.30

Step 2: Prepare your dialogue. Bereitet euer Gespräch vor.

Student A: Choose one of the two cards. Wähle eine der zwei Karten aus.

A
– Du möchtest ein Schinken-Käse-Sandwich und eine Flasche Wasser haben.
– Frage auch nach einem Snack.

B
– Du hast £3.80.
– Überlege, was und wie viel du kaufen möchtest.

> Du kannst deine *shopping phrases* aus den Aufgaben 7 und 8 verwenden.

> Begrüße und verabschiede dich. Sei höflich. Reagiere darauf, was die Bedienung fragt oder sagt.

Student B: Read the card. Take notes.
Lies die Karte. Mach dir Notizen.

Assistant
– Begrüße und verabschiede deine Kundschaft.
– Achte darauf, was die Kundin oder der Kunde fragt. Reagiere höflich darauf.

Step 3: Act the dialogue. Swap roles. Spielt den Dialog. Tauscht die Rollen.

✓ Ich kann Essen und Trinken bestellen.

Picnic snack ideas

1 Watch the film and put the things in the right group.
V 13   Schau dir den Film an und sortiere die Begriffe in die richtige Gruppe.

A lemon B mango C cookies D sugar
E heavy cream F water G cream cheese

Eine Zutat brauchst du zweimal!

cake	drink
cookies	*lemon*

2 Mediation: How can I make it? Wie kann ich es machen?

Suche dir eines der beiden Rezepte aus dem Film aus. Erkläre jemandem aus deiner Klasse oder deiner Familie auf Deutsch, was man für das Rezept benötigt und wie man es macht. Wenn du unsicher bist, schau dir den Film nochmal an.

Hast du Lust, eines dieser Rezepte auszuprobieren? Welches?

✓ Ich kann eine Videoanleitung zu Rezepten verstehen.

6 Reading

Britain and the sea

> **Culture**
>
> Großbritannien ist eine Insel. Als es noch keine Fähren, Tunnel und Flugzeuge gab, konnte man nur mit dem Schiff dorthin kommen. Die Briten waren als erfolgreiche Seefahrer bekannt. Das Meer spielt auch heute im Leben der Menschen dort eine große Rolle.
> Welche Rolle spielt das Meer in deinem Leben?

 A 37

FISH AND CHIPS

Fish and chips are very popular in Britain.
People from Spain and Portugal brought them to Britain a long time ago.
Today you can find a fish and chip shop in a lot of towns in Britain.
People in Britain like to eat fish and chips with salt and vinegar.
A great place to eat fish and chips is on the beach.

 A 38

HOLIDAYS

Seaside towns like Brighton are very popular with tourists.
There are nice beaches but also roller coasters, concerts and shops.

 A 39

THE COAST

In Britain nobody lives more than 125 kilometres from the sea.
The coast of Britain is over 17,000 kilometres long.
It is home to a lot of birds and fish.

Reading 6

1 Read the texts. Lies die Texte.

2 Answer the questions and do the crossword.
Beantworte die Fragen und löse das Kreuzworträtsel.

beaches   Portugal ✓   coast   salt   tourists   nobody

1. Where did fish and chips come from? *Spain and …*
2. What do you eat with them? *… and vinegar*
3. Brighton is very popular with …
4. What can you see there? *nice …*
5. Who lives more than 125 kilometres from the sea? *…*
6. What is home to a lot of fish and birds? *the …*

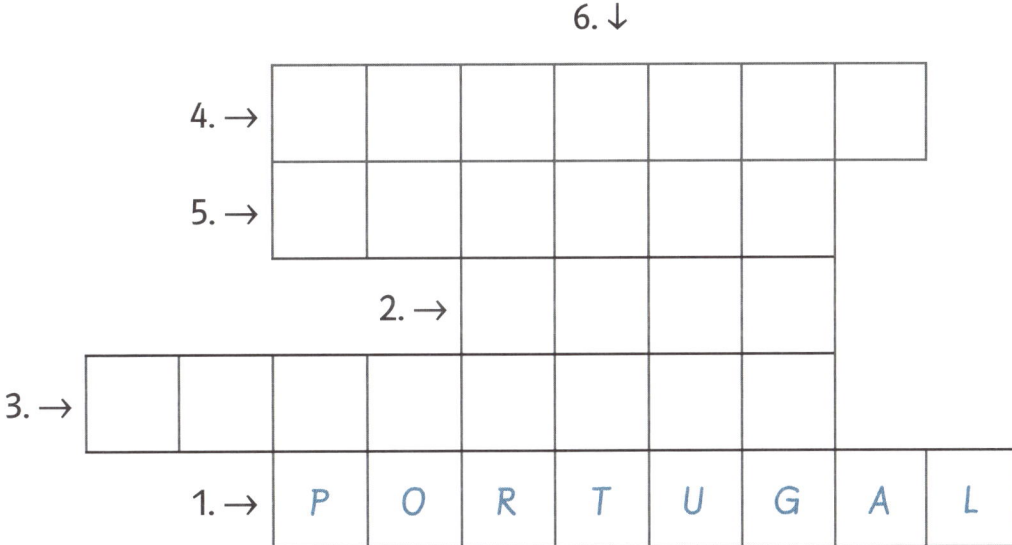

3 Make a poster about a seaside town for your English friend.
Erstelle für deinen englischen Freund ein Poster zu einem Ort am Meer.

Where is it?
near Husum   near Kiel   …

What can you do there?
go to the beach   go cycling   …

What's special about it?
the boats   the snack bars   …

My seaside town
Kühlungsborn (near Rostock)
can go there by train or boat
Tourist train: Molli
Lighthouse in Bastorf

✓ Ich kann Infotexte verstehen.

6 Check out

Task: A quiz

Write questions about topics from your English book. Do a quiz.
Schreibt Fragen über Themen aus eurem Englischbuch. Führt ein Quiz durch.

Step 1:
1. Make five groups (A–E).
Bildet fünf Gruppen (A–E).

2. Each group chooses one topic.
Jede Gruppe wählt ein Thema.

Group A: people in Greenwich
Group B: places in Greenwich
Group C: means of transport
Group D: special days
Group E: Thomas Tallis School

Step 2:
1. Think of five questions in each group.
Denkt euch in jeder Gruppe fünf Fragen aus.

Beispiele:
Group A: Who lives in Brook Lane?
– Katie
Group B: What's the name of a museum in Greenwich?
– the Royal Observatory
Group C: What colour are the buses in Greenwich?
– red
Group D: What's in December?
– Christmas
Group E: Who is Mr Turner?
– the science teacher

> Blättert durch euer Englischbuch und sucht dort nach Informationen. Schreibt eure Stichpunkte und die Lösungen dazu auf.

2. Write the questions and answers.
Schreibt die Fragen und Antworten auf.

Step 3: Do the quiz in class.
Macht das Quiz in eurer Klasse.
1. Die Gruppen stellen der Klasse nacheinander ihre Fragen.
2. Überprüft die Antworten. Welche Gruppe gewinnt?

> Legt fest, wie ihr antworten wollt. Ihr könnt z. B. 30 Sekunden Zeit geben. Jede Gruppe schreibt die Antwort auf einen Zettel und hält ihn nach Ablauf der Zeit hoch.

Discover 6

Six must-see places

1 Look at the photos and read the information.
Schau dir die Fotos an und lies die Informationen dazu.

The Lake District is a beautiful place in England. There are a lot of lakes. It is a perfect place for kayaking.

Cornwall is famous for its beaches and beautiful villages. Visit the Eden Project. You can see banana trees there.

Nottingham is a city with nice shops and cafés. Sherwood Forest, the home of Robin Hood, is near Nottingham.

Dover is at the coast. It has a big castle. The castle stands[1] on some beautiful white cliffs[2].

Stonehenge: Nobody knows who built Stonehenge. It is more than 4,000 years old.

Bodiam Castle is over 600 years old. You can learn about life in the Middle Ages[3] there.

1 to stand – *stehen*; 2 cliff – *die Klippe*; 3 Middle Ages – *das Mittelalter*

2 Which of these places would you like to visit? Why?
Welche dieser Orte würdest du gerne besuchen? Warum?

I'd like to visit … because it is interesting .   cool   a beautiful place   old   …

V Vokabeln Zoom in – Unit 1 – Unit 3 – Unit 5

V1 Numbers 0–12 Zahlen 0–12

0 zero			
1 one	4 four	7 seven	10 ten
2 two	5 five	8 eight	11 eleven
3 three	6 six	9 nine	12 twelve

V2 Colours Farben

black   blue   brown   green   grey

orange   pink   red   white   yellow

V3 Numbers 13–100 Zahlen 13–100

13 thirteen	18 eighteen	30 thirty	70 seventy
14 fourteen	19 nineteen	31 thirty-one	80 eighty
15 fifteen	20 twenty	40 forty	90 ninety
16 sixteen	21 twenty-one	50 fifty	100 a/one hundred
17 seventeen	22 twenty-two	60 sixty	

V4 Ordinal numbers Ordnungszahlen

2nd second   1st first   3rd third

	7th seventh	15th fifteenth
	8th eighth	20th twentieth
	9th ninth	21st twenty-first
	10th tenth	22nd twenty-second
	11th eleventh	23rd twenty-third
4th fourth	12th twelfth	24th twenty-fourth
5th fifth	13th thirteenth	30th thirtieth
6th sixth	14th fourteenth	31st thirty-first

Vokabeln Unit 1

V5 Things for school Dinge für die Schule

1	bag	die Tasche
2	book	das Buch; das Heft
3	exercise book	das Übungsheft
4	folder	die Mappe; der Ordner
5	pen	der Füller; der Stift
6	phone	das Handy; das Telefon
7	tablet	das Tablet
8	uniform	die Uniform

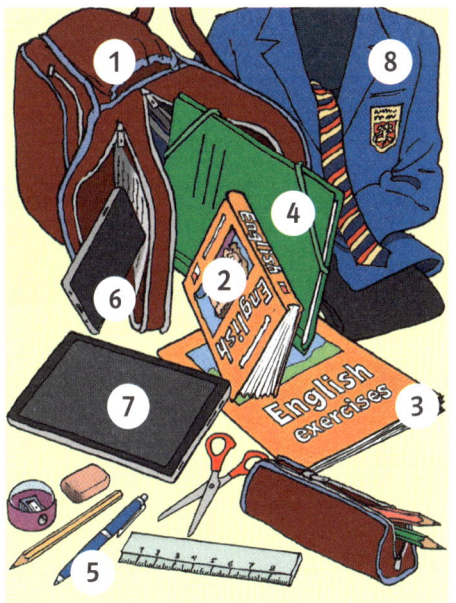

V6 School places Orte in der Schule

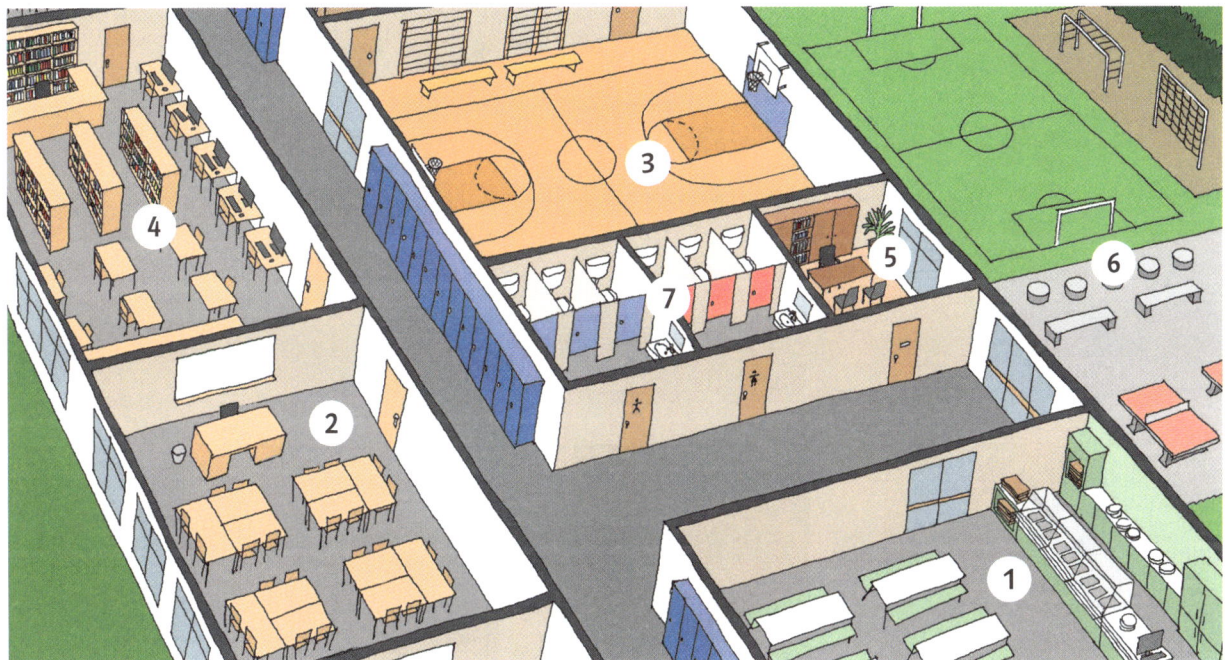

1	cafeteria	die Cafeteria; die Mensa
2	classroom	das Klassenzimmer
3	gym	die Turnhalle
4	library	die Bibliothek; die Bücherei
5	office	das Büro
6	playground	der Schulhof; der Spielplatz
7	toilet	die Toilette

V Vokabeln Unit 1

V7 Days of the week Wochentage

day der Tag week die Woche

Im Englischen schreibst du die meisten Wörter klein, bis auf
- Sprachen *(English, German, …)*
- Wochentage *(Monday, …)*
- Namen *(Emmy, England, …)*
- und *I (Can I have …)*!

V8 School subjects Schulfächer

1

art
Kunst

2

biology
Biologie

3

English
Englisch

5

geography
Geografie

6

German
Deutsch

7

history
Geschichte

8
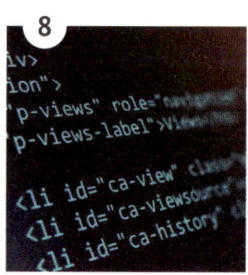
IT
Informatik

9
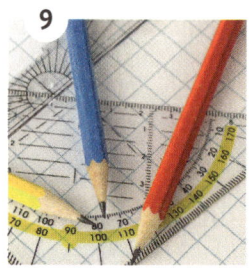
maths
Mathe

10
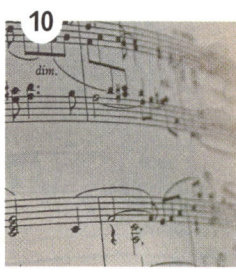
music
Musik

11

PE
Sport

12
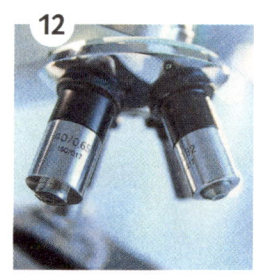
science
Wissenschaft

V9 Family Familie

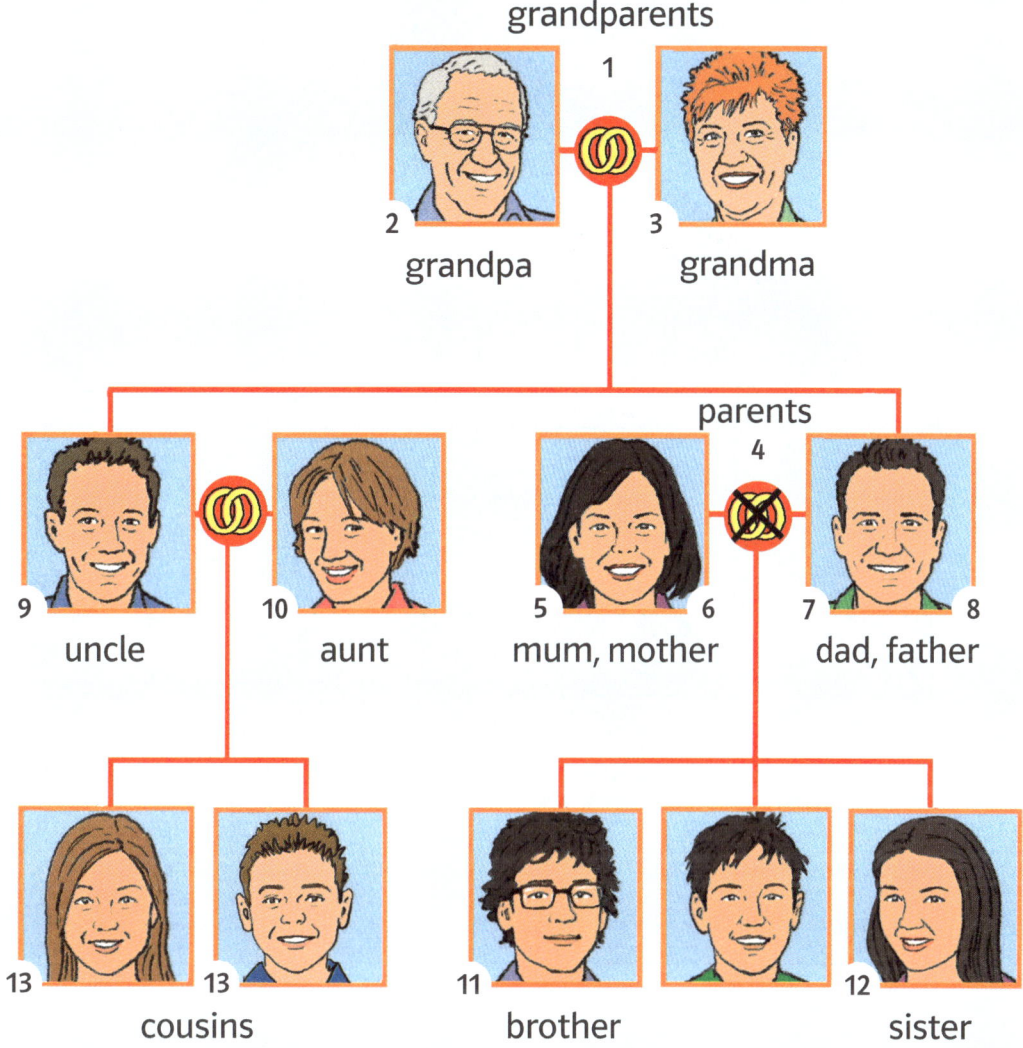

1	grandparents	die Großeltern	9	uncle	der Onkel
2	grandpa	der Opa	10	aunt	die Tante
3	grandma	die Oma	11	brother	der Bruder
4	parents	die Eltern	12	sister	die Schwester
5	mum	die Mama	13	cousin	die Cousine / der Cousin
6	mother	die Mutter			
7	dad	der Papa			
8	father	der Vater			

Vokabeln Unit 2

V10 Rooms Zimmer

1	bathroom	das Badezimmer	4	kitchen	die Küche
2	bedroom	das Schlafzimmer	5	living room	das Wohnzimmer
3	dining room	das Esszimmer	6	room	das Zimmer

Vokabeln Unit 2

V11 Things at home Dinge zu Hause

1	bed	das Bett	7 lamp	die Lampe
2	bin	der Mülleimer	8 picture	das Bild
3	box	die Box; die Kiste; die Schachtel	9 shelf, shelves	das Regal; die Regale
4	chair	der Stuhl	10 sofa	das Sofa
5	cupboard	der Schrank	11 table	der Tisch
6	door	die Tür	12 window	das Fenster

V Vokabeln Unit 3

V12 Free-time activities Freizeitaktivitäten

to do handicrafts
basteln

to do sport
Sport treiben

to go cycling
Fahrrad fahren

to go dancing
tanzen gehen

to go swimming
schwimmen gehen

to meet friends
Freunde treffen

to read books
Bücher lesen

to listen to music
Musik hören

to help in the kitchen
in der Küche helfen

to go to the cinema
ins Kino gehen

to play an instrument
ein Instrument spielen

to play with the dog
mit dem Hund spielen

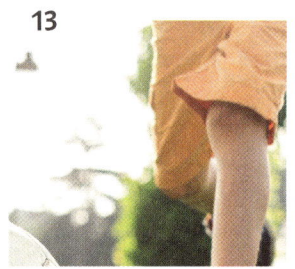
to play football
Fußball spielen

to repair things
Sachen reparieren

to take photos
Fotos machen

to watch films
Filme gucken

V13 Time Zeit

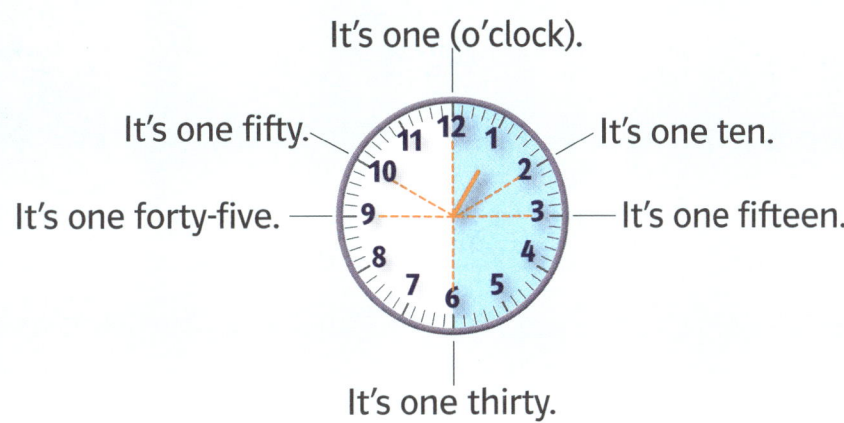

It's one (o'clock).
It's one fifty.
It's one ten.
It's one forty-five.
It's one fifteen.
It's one thirty.

V14 Daily routines Tägliche Abläufe

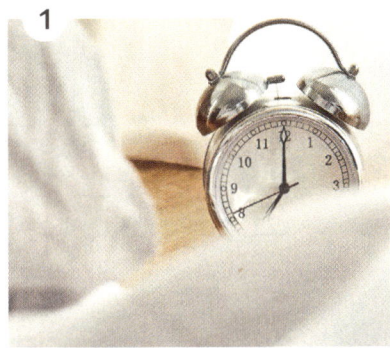

to get up
aufstehen

to have breakfast
frühstücken

to have lunch
zu Mittag essen

to have dinner
zu Abend essen

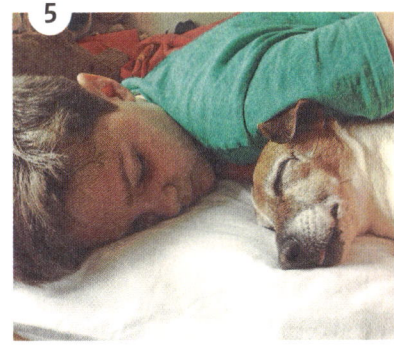

to go to bed
ins Bett gehen

to clean
putzen

V15 Places in town Orte in der Stadt

castle
das Schloss; die Burg

church
die Kirche

market
der Markt

museum
das Musem

park
der Park

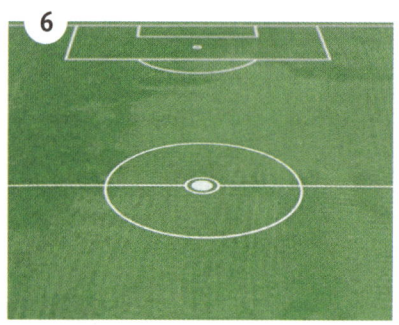
pitch
das Spielfeld; der Platz

river
der Fluss

snack bar
der Imbiss; das Café

supermarket
der Supermarkt

swimming pool
das Schwimmbad

youth club
der Jugendtreff

pond
der Teich

V16 Giving directions Richtungen angeben

into
in; hinein

on the left
auf der linken Seite;
links

on the right
auf der rechten Seite;
rechts

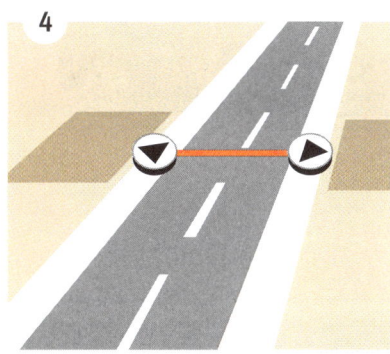

opposite
gegenüber

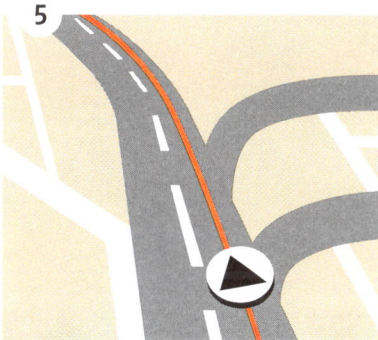

straight on
geradeaus

on the corner
an der Ecke

road
die Straße;
die Landstraße

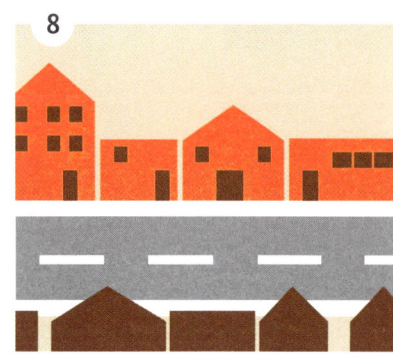

street
die Straße

traffic light
die Ampel

V17 Means of transport Transportmittel

boat
das Boot

bus
der Bus

cable car
die Seilbahn

car
das Auto

on foot
zu Fuß

scooter
der Roller

ship
das Schiff

taxi
das Taxi

V18 Seasons and months Jahreszeiten und Monate

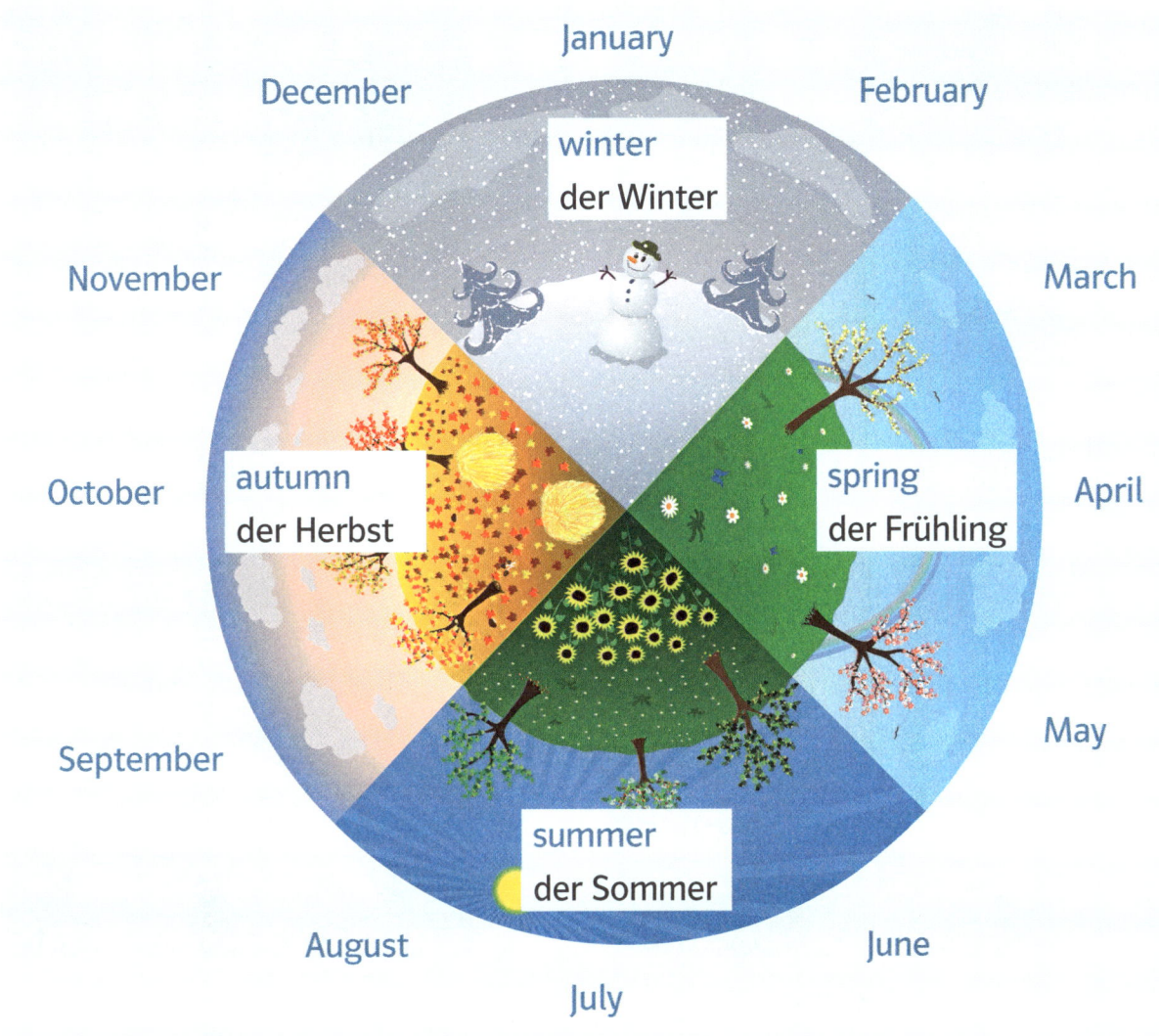

January	Januar	July	Juli
February	Februar	August	August
March	März	September	September
April	April	October	Oktober
May	Mai	November	November
June	Juni	December	Dezember

V19 Weather Wetter

| cloud | die Wolke |
| cloudy | wolkig |

| wind | der Wind |
| windy | windig |

| sun | die Sonne |
| sunny | sonnig |

to rain	regnen
rain	der Regen
rainy	regnerisch

| hot | heiß |
| warm | warm |

| cold | kalt |
| snow | der Schnee |

Vokabeln Unit 6

V20 Food Lebensmittel

apple
der Apfel

banana
die Banane

cheese
der Käse

chips
die Pommes frites

cola
die Cola

crisps
die Chips

drink
das Getränk

egg
das Ei

ham
der Schinken

lemonade
die Limonade

milk
die Milch

orange
die Orange

pasta
die Nudeln

salad
der Salat

tomato, tomatoes
die Tomate

yoghurt
der Joghurt

V21 Quantities Mengen

a bar of chocolate
eine Tafel Schokolade

a bottle of water
eine Flasche Wasser

a can of fish
eine Dose Fisch

a packet of crisps
eine Tüte Chips

1	bar	die Tafel; der Riegel
2	bottle	die Flasche
3	can	die Dose
4	packet	die Packung; die Tüte

A

a	ein / eine
a / one million 1,000,000	eine Million
a / one thousand 1,000	eintausend; tausend
a lot	viel
a.m.	vormittags *(Uhrzeit)*
about	über
activity	Aktivität
ad	Werbung; Anzeige
adult	Erwachsener / Erwachsene
adventure	Abenteuer
after	nach
afternoon	Nachmittag
again	noch einmal; wieder
ago	vor *(zeitlich)*
all	alle; alles; ganz
also	auch
always	immer
am	bin
an	ein / eine
and	und
angry	wütend; verärgert; böse
animal	Tier
another	ein anderer / eine andere; noch ein
Anything else?	Darf es sonst noch etwas sein?
apple	Apfel
April	April
are	bist / sind / seid
aren't (= are not)	bist / sind / seid nicht
around	rund um; um … herum
to arrive	ankommen
arrow	Pfeil
art	Kunst
to ask	fragen; bitten
assistant	Verkäufer / Verkäuferin
astronaut	Astronaut / Astronautin
at	in; an; um; bei; auf
at home	zu Hause
August	August
aunt	Tante
autumn	Herbst

B

back	zurück
bad	schlecht; böse
bag	Tasche; Tüte
ball	Ball
banana	Banane
bar	Tafel; Riegel
bathroom	Badezimmer; Bad
to be	sein
to be fun	Spaß machen
to be good at	gut sein in
beach	Strand
bear	Bär
beautiful	schön; hübsch
bed	Bett
bedroom	Schlafzimmer; Kinderzimmer
behind	hinter
big	groß
bike	Fahrrad
bin	Mülleimer
biology	Biologie
bird	Vogel
birthday	Geburtstag
board	Tafel
boat	Boot
book	Buch; Heft
boring	langweilig
to borrow	ausleihen

Wörterbuch

bottle	Flasche
box	Box; Kiste; Schachtel
boy	Junge
break	Pause
breakfast	Frühstück
to bring, brought	bringen, brachte; mitbringen, brachte mit
Britain	Großbritannien
brother	Bruder
bus	Bus
busy	belebt; beschäftigt
but	aber
to buy, bought	kaufen, kaufte
by (bike)	mit (dem Fahrrad)
Bye.	Tschüss.

C

cable car	Seilbahn
café	Café
cafeteria	Cafeteria; Mensa
cake	Kuchen
to call	anrufen; rufen
camp	Camp; Lager
can	können
Can you help me?	Können Sie mir helfen?; Kannst du mir helfen?
Can you spell that?	Kannst du das buchstabieren?
can't (= cannot)	nicht können
candle	Kerze
cap	Mütze; Kappe
car	Auto
car park	Parkplatz
castle	Schloss; Burg
cat	Katze
cave	Höhle
centre	Zentrum; Center
chair	Stuhl

change	Wechselgeld; Restgeld
to chat	chatten; plaudern
check in	Einchecken
check out	Auschecken
cheeky	frech
cheese	Käse
children	Kinder
chips	Pommes frites
chocolate	Schokolade
chorus	Refrain
Christmas	Weihnachten
church	Kirche
cinema	Kino
city	Stadt; Großstadt
class	Klasse; Unterricht; Unterrichtsstunde
classroom	Klassenzimmer
to clean	sauber machen; putzen
climbing	Klettern
climbing wall	Kletterwand
to close	schließen; zumachen
cloud	Wolke
cloudy	wolkig
club	Klub; Schul-AG
coast	Küste
cola	Cola
cold	kalt
to collect	einsammeln; sammeln
colour	Farbe
to come, came	kommen, kam
to come in	hereinkommen
computer	Computer
concert	Konzert
cookie	Keks
cool	cool; super; kühl
corner	Ecke
to cost	kosten
cousin	Cousin / Cousine

cow	Kuh
crazy	verrückt
cream	Sahne; Rahm; Creme
cream cheese	Frischkäse
criminal	Kriminieller / Kriminelle; Verbrecher / Verbrecherin
crisp	Kartoffelchip
to cross	überqueren
cucumber	Gurke
culture	Kultur
cupboard	Schrank
cycling	Radfahren

D

dad	Papa
daily	täglich; Alltags-
dance	Tanz-; Tanz
dangerous	gefährlich
date	Datum
day	Tag
December	Dezember
difficult	schwierig
dining room	Esszimmer
dinner	Abendessen
to do, did	machen, machte; tun, tat
to do handicrafts	basteln
to do sport	Sport treiben
dog	Hund
Don't talk.	Sei(d) still.; Rede(t) nicht.
door	Tür
down	herunter; hinunter; entlang; (nach) unten
dress	Kleid
drink	Getränk
to drink, drank	trinken, trank

E

earth	Erde; Boden
easy	einfach; leicht
to eat, ate	essen, aß
egg	Ei
England	England
English	Englisch; englisch; aus England
evening	Abend
every	jede / jeder / jedes
everyone	jede / jeder / jedes
exam	Prüfung
excited	aufgeregt
Excuse me!	Entschuldigung!
exercise book	Übungsheft
experiment	Experiment

F

fairground	Rummelplatz
family	Familie
famous	berühmt
fan	Fan
farm	Bauernhof
fast	schnell
father	Vater
favourite	Lieblings-
February	Februar
to feed	füttern
film	Film
to find	finden; herausfinden
fine	schön; fein
fireworks	Feuerwerk
fish, fish	Fisch, Fische
flat	Wohnung
folder	Ordner; Mappe
foot	Fuß
football	Fußball
for	für

forest	Wald
form	Form
to free	befreien
free	kostenlos; frei
free time	Freizeit
free-time	Freizeit-
Friday	Freitag
fridge	Kühlschrank
friend	Freund / Freundin
frog	Frosch
from	von; aus
fun	Spaß; Freude
funny	lustig; witzig; komisch; merkwürdig; seltsam

G

game	Spiel
garden	Garten
geography	Erdkunde; Geografie
Germany	Deutschland
to get around	herumkommen
to get up	aufstehen
to get, got	werden, wurde; bekommen, bekam
girl	Mädchen
to go cycling	Fahrrad fahren
to go dancing	tanzen gehen
to go shopping	einkaufen gehen
to go swimming	schwimmen gehen
to go walking	spazieren gehen; wandern gehen
to go, went	gehen, ging; fahren, fuhr
goal	Tor; Ziel
gold	Gold
good	gut
Good morning.	Guten Morgen.
Goodbye.	Auf Wiedersehen.

gorilla	Gorilla
grandma	Oma
grandpa	Opa
grandparents	Großeltern
great	toll; großartig; groß
group	Gruppe
gym	Turnhalle; Fitnessstudio

H

hair	Haar; Haare
ham	Schinken
hand	Hand
handicraft	Handarbeit
happy	glücklich
has	hat
hat	Hut
to have, had	haben, hatte
he	er
he's (= he is)	er ist
heavy	schwer; stark
heavy cream	Sahne mit sehr hohem Fettgehalt
Hello there.	Hallo.; Grüß dich.
Hello.	Hallo.
to help	helfen
help	Hilfe
her	ihr / ihre; sie
here	hier
Here you are.	Bitte schön.
hero	Held / Heldin
Hey!	Hey!
Hi.	Hi.; Hallo.
high street	Hauptstraße
him	ihm; ihn
his	sein / seine
history	Geschichte
holiday	Ferien; Urlaub; Feiertag
home	Zuhause; Heim

homework	Hausaufgabe, Hausaufgaben	**J**	
horse	Pferd	jam	Marmelade; Konfitüre
hot	heiß	January	Januar
house	Haus	jewellery	Schmuck
how	wie	juice	Saft
How are you?	Wie geht es dir?	July	Juli
How much (is/are) …?	Wie viel (kostet/kosten) …?	to jump	springen
		to jump in	reinspringen
How old are you?	Wie alt bist du?	June	Juni
hungry	hungrig	**K**	
I		kangaroo	Känguru
I	ich	kayaking	Kajakfahren
I don't like …	Ich mag … nicht; … gefällt mir nicht.	kid	Kind
		kilometre	Kilometer
I'd like … (= I would like)	Ich hätte gerne …; Ich möchte gerne …; Ich würde gerne …	king	König
		kitchen	Küche
		L	
I'm (= I am)	ich bin	lake	See
I'm from …	Ich komme aus …	lamp	Lampe
I'm sorry.	Es tut mir leid.	language	Sprache
ice cream	Eiscreme; Eis	last	letzte / letzter / letztes
ice skating	Schlittschuhlaufen	late	spät; zu spät
idea	Idee; Ahnung	later	später
iguana	Leguan	to learn	erfahren; herausfinden; lernen
in	in		
in front of	vor; davor	to leave	abfahren; verlassen; lassen
in the evening(s)	abends		
		left	links
instrument	Instrument	leg	Bein
interesting	interessant	lemon	Zitrone
into	in; hinein	lemonade	Limonade
is	ist	lesson	Schulstunde
isn't (= is not)	ist nicht	let's (= let us)	lass(t) uns
it	es	library	Bibliothek; Bücherei
IT (= Information Technology)	Informatik	life	Leben
		light	Licht
it's (= it is)	er / sie / es ist	lighthouse	Leuchtturm

Wörterbuch

to like	mögen
lion	Löwe
to listen (to)	zuhören; anhören; hören
listening	Hörverstehen
to live	wohnen; leben
living room	Wohnzimmer
long	lang; lange
to look	sehen; aussehen
to look at	anschauen
to love	lieben; gern mögen
lunch	Mittagessen
lunchbox	Brotdose

M

magic	magisch; Zauber-
to make, made	machen, machte; tun, tat
man, men	Mann, Männer
mango	Mango
many	viele
March	März
market	Markt
maths	Mathematik; Mathe
May	Mai
Mayan	Maya
me	mich; mir
means of transport	Transportmittel; Verkehrsmittel
media	Medien-; Medien
mediation	Sprachmittlung
to meet	treffen; kennenlernen
to milk	melken
milk	Milch
minute	Minute
mix	Mischung
Monday	Montag
more	mehr; weitere
morning	Morgen; Vormittag
mother	Mutter
mountain	Berg
mouse	Maus
Mr	Herr (Anrede)
Mrs	Frau (Anrede)
Ms	Frau (Anrede)
much	viel
mum	Mama
museum	Museum
music	Musik
must	müssen
my	mein / meine
My name is …	Ich heiße …

N

name	Name
near	in der Nähe von
to need	brauchen
needle	Nadel
neighbour	Nachbar / Nachbarin
nervous	nervös
never	nie; niemals
new	neu
New Year	Neujahr
news	Nachrichten; Neuigkeiten
next to	neben
nice	schön; nett
Nice to meet you.	Schön, dich kennenzulernen.
Nigeria	Nigeria
night	Nacht; Abend
no	nein; kein / keine
nobody	niemand
not	nicht
November	November
now	jetzt; nun

number	Zahl; Nummer; Anzahl

O

o'clock	Uhr *(Zeitangabe bei vollen Stunden)*
ocean	Ozean; Meer
October	Oktober
of	von
of course	natürlich; selbstverständlich
office	Büro
often	oft; häufig
OK	okay
old	alt
on	an; auf
on foot	zu Fuß
on the left	auf der linken Seite; links
one another	einander; gegenseitig
only	nur
to open	öffnen; aufmachen
open	geöffnet; offen
opposite	gegenüber
or	oder
orange	Orange
organic	Bio-; organisch
our	unser / unsere
out and about	unterwegs
outside	nach draußen; draußen
over	über
own	eigene / eigener / eigenes

P

p.m.	nachmittags *(Uhrzeit)*
packet	Packung; Tüte
pancake	Pfannkuchen; Eierkuchen
pardon	Entschuldigung
parents	Eltern
park	Park
part	Gegend; Teil
party	Party; Feier
past	vorbei (an)
pasta	Nudeln; Pasta
PE (= Physical Education)	Sportunterricht
pen	Füller; Stift
people	Leute; Menschen
pepper	Paprika; Paprikaschote; Pfeffer
pet	Haustier
phone	Handy; Telefon
photo	Foto
picnic	Picknick
picture	Bild
pig	Schwein
pitch	Spielfeld; Platz
pizza	Pizza
place	Ort; Platz; Stelle
to plan	planen
platform	Bahnsteig
to play	spielen
playground	Schulhof; Spielplatz
please	bitte
police	Polizei
pond	Teich
popular	beliebt
Portugal	Portugal
potion	Trank
pound	Pfund *(brit. Währungseinheit)*
present	Geschenk
proud (of)	stolz (auf)

Q

queen	Königin
question	Frage
quiet	leise; still; ruhig

R

race	Wettrennen; Rennen
radio	Radio
to rain	regnen
rain	Regen
rainy	regnerisch
rat	Ratte
to read, read	lesen, las
reading	Lesen
recording	Aufnahme
recording studio	Tonstudio
registration	Anwesenheitskontrolle
to remember	sich erinnern (an); sich merken
to repair	reparieren
restaurant	Restaurant
to ride, rode	fahren, fuhr; reiten, ritt
right	rechts
river	Fluss
road	Straße
roller coaster	Achterbahn
room	Zimmer; Raum; Platz
routine	Routine; Ablauf
rule	Regel
to run, ran	laufen, lief; rennen, rann

S

safe	in Sicherheit; sicher
salad	Salat
sale	Verkauf; Ausverkauf
salt	Salz
sandwich	Sandwich; belegtes Brot
Saturday	Samstag
to say, said	sagen, sagte; sprechen, sprach
scary	gruselig
school	Schule
science	Wissenschaft; Naturwissenschaft
sea	Meer
seaside	Küste; Küsten-
season	Jahreszeit; Saison
See you later.	Tschüss.; Bis bald.
to see, saw	sehen, sah
September	September
to share	teilen
she	sie
she's (= she is)	sie ist
shelf, shelves	Regal, Regale; Regalbrett, Regalbretter
ship	Schiff
shirt	Shirt
shoe	Schuh
shop	Laden; Geschäft
shopping	Einkaufen
shopping centre	Einkaufszentrum
short	kurz
silly	blöd; dumm; albern
sister	Schwester
to sit down	sich hinsetzen; sich setzen
skate park	Skatepark
skateboard	Skateboard
skill	Fähigkeit; Kenntnis; Fertigkeit
skirt	Rock
to sleep, slept	schlafen, schlief
slow	langsam
small	klein
smart	schlau; intelligent; gepflegt; schick
snack	Snack; Imbiss
snack bar	Café; Imbissstube
snake	Schlange
snow	Schnee

so	so; also; daher	survey	Umfrage
sofa	Sofa	swimming	Schwimmen
some	ein paar; einige; manche	swimming pool	Schwimmbad
sometimes	manchmal	sword	Schwert
Sorry.	Tut mir leid.; Entschuldigung.		

T

space	Weltraum; der Platz	table	Tisch
space station	Raumstation	tablet	Tablet
Spain	Spanien	to take, took	(mit-)nehmen, nahm (mit); dauern, dauerte
special	besonders; speziell	to take out	herausnehmen; herausbringen
to spell	buchstabieren	to take photos	fotografieren; Fotos machen
to spend, spent	verbringen, verbrachte; ausgeben *(Geld)*, gab aus	Take that!	Nimm das!
sport	Sport; Sportart	to talk (to)	sprechen (mit); reden (mit)
spring	Frühling; Frühjahr	task	Aufgabe; Auftrag
to start	anfangen; beginnen; starten	taxi	Taxi
station	Station; Bahnhof	teacher	Lehrer / Lehrerin
to stay	bleiben; übernachten	to tell	sagen; erzählen
step	Schritt	tent	Zelt
to stop	anhalten; stehen bleiben; stoppen; aufhören	than	als
Stop it!	Hör(t) auf!	Thank you.	Danke.
straight on	geradeaus	that	der / die / das
street	Straße	That's £4.40.	Das macht vier Pfund und 40 Pence.
student	Schüler / Schülerin; Student / Studentin	the	der; die *(auch Pl.)*; das
studio	Studio; Atelier	their	ihr *(Pl.)*; ihre *(Pl.)*
subject	Schulfach	them	sie *(Pl.)*; ihnen
sugar	Zucker	then	danach; dann
summer	Sommer	there	da; dort
sun	Sonne	there are	da sind; es gibt
Sunday	Sonntag	there is	da ist; dort ist; es gibt
sunny	sonnig	these	das; diese (hier)
supermarket	Supermarkt	they	sie *(Pl.)*
support	Hilfe; Unterstützung	they're (= they are)	sie sind
surprised	überrascht	thing	Sache; Ding

Wörterbuch

to think	finden; denken; glauben
this	das; dies
Thursday	Donnerstag
ticket	Fahrkarte; Eintrittskarte
ticket office	Fahrkartenschalter
time	Uhrzeit; Zeit; Mal
tip	Tipp; Ratschlag
tired	müde
to	in; zu; nach; bis
today	heute
together	zusammen; gemeinsam
toilet	Toilette
tomato	Tomate
too	auch; zu
top	Top; Oberteil
tour	Rundgang; Tour; Reise
tourist	Tourist / Touristin
tourist information centre	Touristeninformation
town	Stadt
toy	Spielzeug
train	Zug
train	der Bahnhof
tree	Baum
trip	Fahrt; Trip; Ausflug; Reise
Tuesday	Dienstag
to turn	abbiegen; drehen
tutor	Klassenlehrer / Klassenlehrerin
tutor time	Klassenstunde

U

umbrella	Regenschirm
uncle	Onkel
under	unter
uniform	Uniform
us	uns; wir

V

vacuum cleaner	Staubsauger
very	sehr
video	Video
viewing	Sehen
village	Dorf
vinegar	Essig
violin	Geige
to visit	besuchen

W

wall	Wand; Mauer
to want (to)	wollen
warm	warm
was	war
to watch	anschauen; ansehen; beobachten
water	Wasser
way	Weg
we	wir
we're (= we are)	wir sind
weather	Wetter
Wednesday	Mittwoch
week	Woche
weekend	Wochenende
welcome (to)	willkommen (bei / in)
were	waren
what	was; wie; welche
What about …?	Was ist mit …?
What time is it?	Wie spät ist es?
what's (= what is)	was ist
What's your name?	Wie heißt du?
when	wann
where	wo; wohin; woher

Where are you from?	Woher kommst du?	**Y**	
		yak	Yak
which	der / die / das; dem; den	**year**	Klasse; Jahrgangsstufe; Jahr
why	warum		
wind	Wind	**yes**	ja
window	Fenster	**yesterday**	gestern
windy	windig	**yoghurt**	Joghurt
winter	Winter	**you**	du; dir; dich; ihr; euch; Sie; Ihnen
with	mit		
word	Wort	**You're welcome.**	Gern geschehen.
to work	arbeiten		
would like	würde(n) gern; hätte(n) gern	**your**	dein / deine; euer / eure; Ihr / Ihre
to write	schreiben	**Your turn.**	Du bist dran.
		youth club	Jugendtreff
X		**Z**	
xylophone	Xylophon	**zebra**	Zebra
		zoo	Zoo; Tierpark
		zoom in	Heranzoomen

Quellennachweis

Ablang, Friederike, Berlin, **12,1.7**; **5,2.7**; Assies, Juliane, Berlin, **7,1.1**; Avenue Images GmbH, Hamburg (Stockbyte), **126.11**; Bláha, Marek, Offenbach am Main, **5.3**; **7.1**; **8.1**; **8.2**; **9.1**; **9.2**; **9.3**; **9.4**; **11.1**; **13.8**; **13.15**; **15.1**; **19.1**; **20.1**; **20.2**; **21.1**; **29.3**; **31.1**; **33.1**; **33.2**; **36.7**; **37.2**; **38.1**; **38.2**; **39.1**; **39.8**; **42.1**; **42.2**; **42.3**; **42.4**; **42.5**; **42.6**; **42.7**; **42.8**; **43.1**; **43.2**; **47.1**; **49.1**; **49.2**; **50.1**; **50.2**; **55.1**; **55.2**; **56.1**; **57.1**; **59.9**; **60.1**; **60.2**; **60.3**; **60.4**; **62.1**; **68.2**; **69.1**; **71.5**; **75.1**; **75.3**; **77.7**; **77.8**; **83.5**; **86.1**; **87.1**; **88.1**; **92.1**; **93.1**; **96.1**; **96.2**; **96.3**; **103.1**; **104.1**; **104.2**; **105.1**; **108.2**; **112.2**; **113.8**; **113.9**; **116.1**; **116.2**; **120.5**; **1,2.1**; **11,1.1**; **11,1.2**; **11,1.3**; **11,1.4**; **11,1.5**; **6,1.1**; **7,1.4**; Boncompagni, Athos, Arezzo Italy, **4.3**; Brüggemann, Vera, Bielefeld, **12,1.6**; Chudinskiy, Kirill, Köln, **13.9**; **13.10**; **13.11**; **13.12**; **13.13**; **13.14**; **14.1**; **14.2**; **14.3**; **14.4**; **15.3**; **15.4**; **15.5**; **15.6**; **15.7**; **15.8**; **36.1**; **37.1**; **38.3**; **38.4**; **86.2**; **90.1**; **90.2**; **90.3**; **90.4**; **92.2**; **92.3**; **92.4**; **95.1**; **95.2**; **105.2**; **107.5**; **107.6**; **107.7**; **107.8**; **107.9**; **107.10**; **108.1**; **110.1**; **111.1**; **7,1.3**; **7,1.11**; Corbis RF, Berlin, **128.8**; Corel Corporation Deutschland, Unterschleissheim, **101.1**; creativ collection Verlag GmbH, Freiburg, **13.7**; Dekelver, Christian, Weinstadt, **7,1.9**; Ernst Klett Verlag GmbH, Stuttgart, **4.4**; **7,1.2**; Fosseway Films Ltd., London (Andrea Artz), **4.1**; **4.2**; **5.1**; **5.2**; **10.1**; **10.2**; **10.3**; **10.4**; **12.1**; **12.2**; **12.3**; **12.4**; **12.6**; **12.7**; **18.1**; **21.2**; **24.1**; **24.2**; **24.3**; **24.4**; **24.5**; **24.6**; **28.1**; **28.2**; **29.1**; **39.3**; **46.1**; **46.2**; **46.3**; **46.4**; **48.2**; **61.1**; **64.2**; **82.1**; **82.2**; **100.1**; **124.9**; **2,1.1**; **2,1.2**; **2,1.3**; **8,1.3**; Fröhlich, Anke, Leipzig, **12,1.2**; Getty Images Plus, München (Adam Calaitzis), **78.4**; Getty Images Plus, München (Alena Kravchenko), **81.5**; Getty Images Plus, München (anyaivanova), **91.2**; **130.3**; Getty Images Plus, München (Baks/iStock), **78.5**; Getty Images Plus, München (barmalini), **131.3**; Getty Images Plus, München (beats3 iStock), **89.4**; Getty Images Plus, München (beats3), **131.5**; Getty Images Plus, München (BreatheFitness), **71.3**; Getty Images Plus, München (CGinspiration), **120.7**; Getty Images Plus, München (Chris Hepburn), **117.3**; Getty Images Plus, München (ClaireLucia), **131.6**; Getty Images Plus, München (ClarkandCompany), **19.4**; Getty Images Plus, München (coldsnowstorm), **68.1**; Getty Images Plus, München (Csaba Toth), **102.2**; Getty Images Plus, München (c11yg), **131.1**; Getty Images Plus, München (Daly and Newton), **67.2**; **126.9**; Getty Images Plus, München (davidf), **125.2**; Getty Images Plus, München (DenKuvaiev), **28.3**; **8,1.1**; Getty Images Plus, München (Drbouz), **131.10**; Getty Images Plus, München (EllenMoran), **17.7**; Getty Images Plus, München (FangXiaNuo), **73.8**; Getty Images Plus, München (fstop123), **30.2**; Getty Images Plus, München (fusaromike), **120.11**; Getty Images Plus, München (Fuse), **31.3**; Getty Images Plus, München (Gary John Norman), **17.5**; Getty Images Plus, München (georgeclerk), **59.8**; **81.1**; Getty Images Plus, München (gipi23), **17.3**; Getty Images Plus, München (gollykim), **125.5**; Getty Images Plus, München (graletta), **125.3**; Getty Images Plus, München (Guerilla), **59.2**; Getty Images Plus, München (hidesy), **107.3**; Getty Images Plus, München (IllustratedFritz), **120.12**; Getty Images Plus, München (Imgorthand), **124.14**; Getty Images Plus, München (inese online), **131.13**; Getty Images Plus, München (JackF), **132.3**; Getty Images Plus, München (JamesBrey), **81.6**; Getty Images Plus, München (jessicaphoto), **117.5**; Getty Images Plus, München (Julia_Sudnitskaya), **91.3**; **130.4**; Getty Images Plus, München (kali9), **30.5**; **124.6**; Getty Images Plus, München (Karen M. Romanko), **84.3**; Getty Images Plus, München (Karisssa), **131.16**; Getty Images Plus, München (Klaus Vedfelt), **30.1**; Getty Images Plus, München (KOEUTH PHEAP), **120.8**; Getty Images Plus, München (kokouu), **124.1**; Getty Images Plus, München (LauriPatterson), **131.4**; Getty Images Plus, München (lesichkadesign/iStock), **102.1**; Getty Images Plus, München (LightFieldStudios), **124.2**; Getty Images Plus, München (Lucy Lambriex), **36.5**; Getty Images Plus, München (Luis Alvarez), **47.5**; Getty Images Plus, München (Madzia71), **120.3**; Getty Images Plus, München (Marc Dufresne), **106.1**; Getty Images Plus, München (Martin Leitch), **71.1**; Getty Images Plus, München (MesquitaFMS), **124.7**; Getty Images Plus, München (mikanaka), **120.6**; Getty Images Plus, München (mixetto), **47.3**; Getty Images Plus, München (monkeybusinessimages), **124.10**; **124.12**; Getty Images Plus, München (Natalia Van Doninck), **89.1**; Getty Images Plus, München (NERYX), **131.2**; Getty Images Plus, München (NicolasMcComber), **64.5**; Getty Images Plus, München (nicolas_), **120.13**; Getty Images Plus, München (nycshooter), **91.5**; Getty Images Plus, München (Obak), **131.11**; Getty Images Plus, München (Oleksandr Kuznetsov), **131.12**; Getty Images Plus, München (Olga Niekrasova), **91.4**; **130.6**; Getty Images Plus, München (PeopleImages), **59.6**; **124.11**; Getty Images Plus, München (Peter Dazeley), **23.2**; **41.3**; **41.9**; Getty Images Plus, München (peterschreiber.media), **120.4**; Getty Images Plus, München (Photodisc/Donna Day), **31.2**; **39.5**; Getty Images Plus, München (pinkomelet), **131.7**; Getty Images Plus, München (RasselOK), **91.8**; Getty Images Plus, München (Ratchat), **132.2**; Getty Images Plus, München (Rifka Hayati), **128.6**; Getty Images Plus, München (romrodinka), **74.8**; **107.1**; Getty Images Plus, München (Sally Anscombe), **84.6**; **99.3**; Getty Images Plus, München (Sanny11 iStock), **131.8**; Getty Images Plus, München (sarymsakov), **125.6**; Getty Images Plus, München (scanrail), **120.9**; Getty Images Plus, München (SDI Productions), **Cover.1**; Getty Images Plus, München (Serbogachuk), **131.15**; Getty Images Plus, München (Silvrshootr iStock), **17.6**; Getty Images Plus, München (StockPlanets), **82.3**; **124.13**; Getty Images Plus, München (svariophoto), **125.4**; Getty Images Plus, München (Tolga_TEZCAN), **77.1**; Getty Images Plus, München (tommaso79), **107.2**; Getty Images Plus, München (Tooga), **53.2**; Getty Images Plus, München (ugurhan), **131.9**; Getty Images Plus, München (vikif), **109.7**; Getty Images Plus, München (Westhoff), **87.2**; Getty Images Plus, München (yotrak), **91.1**; Getty Images Plus, München (Zave Smith), **61.3**; Getty Images RF, München (Photo Disc), **82.5**; Getty Images RF, München (Photodisc), **82.4**; Getty Images, München (Abdul Aziz / EyeEm), **63.3**; Getty Images, München (Adam Foster), **79.1**; Getty Images, München (Aleksandr Zubkov), **39.4**; Getty Images, München (Alexandra C. Ribeiro), **13.1**; Getty Images, München (Andy Nathan / EyeEm), **36.6**; Getty Images, München (Cavan Images), **88.2**; Getty Images, München (Corbis/VCG), **63.2**; Getty Images, München (Creatas Video+ / Sergo2), **53.3**; Getty Images, München (Cyndi Monaghan), **36.2**; Getty Images, München (Daniel Allan), **81.3**; Getty Images, München (David Madison), **63.6**; Getty Images, München (Emma Gibbs), **81.4**; Getty Images, München (Ezra Bailey), **67.1**; **126.8**; Getty Images, München (Fabian Krause / EyeEm), **81.2**; Getty Images, München (Georgy Kuznetsov / EyeEm), **117.2**; Getty Images, München (Giulia Fiori Photography), **117.4**; Getty Images, München (Guy Vanderelst), **81.8**; Getty Images, München (Hiroshi Watanabe), **78.3**; Getty Images, München (Ivan), **84.1**; Getty Images, München (Jack Taylor), **45.3**; Getty Images, München (jayk7), **99.2**; Getty Images, München (JONATHAN BRADY/POOL/AFP), **45.2**; Getty Images, München (Jurgita Vaicikeviciene / EyeEm), **7.2**; Getty Images, München (Landscapes, Seascapes, Jewellery & Action Photographer), **114.4**; Getty Images, München (Maskot), **59.4**; Getty Images, München (Michael Loccisano), **53.1**; Getty Images, München (Monty Rakusen), **114.2**; Getty Images, München (Photograph by Devon OpdenDries.), **36.4**; Getty Images, München (Reinhard Krull / EyeEm), **81.7**; Getty Images, München (Robin Gentry / EyeEm), **30.4**; Getty Images, München (Sharon Vos-Arnold), **59.7**; Getty Images, München (Steve Glass), **117.1**; Getty Images, München (Stockbyte), **64.4**; Getty Images, München (Thorsten Nilson / EyeEm), **39.6**; Getty Images, München (Travelpix Ltd), **59.5**; Getty Images, München (Utamaru Kido), **13.4**; Getty Images, München (Westend61), **30.6**; **67.3**; **91.6**; **114.3**; Getty Images, München (Zero Creatives), **126.10**; Hesselbarth, Susann, Leipzig, **118.1**; **118.2**; **118.3**; **118.4**; **118.5**; **118.6**; **118.7**; **118.8**; **118.9**; **118.10**; **5,1.3**; Hochmann, Carmen, Gütersloh, **118.11**; Hoppe-Engbring, Yvonne, Steinfurt, **7,1.5**; h3-12-007501-0001, **5,2.5**; **5,2.6**; iStockphoto, Calgary, Alberta (bhofack2), **132.1**; iStockphoto, Calgary, Alberta (gradyreese), **54.3**; iStockphoto, Calgary, Alberta (nensuria), **101.2**; iStockphoto, Calgary, Alberta (oneinchpunch), **124.15**; iStockphoto, Calgary, Alberta (RF), **130.5**; iStockphoto, Calgary, Alberta (rotofrank), **126.6**; iStockphoto, Calgary, Alberta (yenwen), **101.4**; Jähde, Steffen, Sundhagen, **5,1.1**; **7,1.8**; jani lunablau, Barcelona, **74.1**; **74.2**; **74.3**; **83.1**; **83.2**; **83.3**; **83.4**; **95.3**; **95.4**; **95.5**; **95.6**; **95.7**; **95.8**; **97.1**; **97.2**; **97.3**; **97.4**; **97.5**; Kranenberg, Hendrik, Drolshagen, **4.7**; **12,1.1**; **12,1.8**; **3,1.4**; **3,1.6**; **5,1.2**; **5,2.2**; **5,2.3**; **7,1.6**; Kreye, Heike, Hamburg, **3,1.1**; **3,1.5**; Leberer, Sven, Altenberge, **19.6**; **19.7**; **19.8**; **19.9**; **19.10**; **19.11**; **19.12**; Mauritius Images, Mittenwald (Arcaid Images / Alamy), **28.5**; **8,1.4**; Mauritius Images, Mittenwald (A.P.S. (UK)/Alamy), **59.1**; Mauritius Images, Mittenwald (Bob Daemmrich / Alamy), **27.3**; Mauritius Images, Mittenwald (BRIAN ANTHONY / Alamy), **74.9**; Mauritius Images, Mittenwald (By Ian Miles-Flashpoint Pictures/Alamy), **27.1**; Mauritius Images, Mittenwald (Ceri Breeze / Alamy), **74.6**; Mauritius Images, Mittenwald (Ian Dagnall / Alamy), **64.3**; Mauritius Images, Mittenwald (ICIMAGE / Alamy), **114.1**; Mauritius Images, Mittenwald (J. Schwanke/Alamy), **115.1**; Mauritius Images, Mittenwald (Kumar Sriskandan/Alamy), **100.5**; Mauritius Images, Mittenwald (Londonstills.com/ Alamy), **100.2**; Mauritius Images, Mittenwald (Mike Hughes / Alamy), **71.2**; Mauritius Images, Mittenwald (Nick Moore / Alamy), **100.3**; Mauritius Images, Mittenwald (one-image photography / Alamy), **74.7**; Mauritius Images, Mittenwald (Paul Melling / Alamy), **100.4**; Mauritius Images, Mittenwald (peter jordan / Alamy), **74.5**; Mauritius Images, Mittenwald (Piero Cruciatti / Alamy), **89.5**; Mauritius Images, Mittenwald (Radharc Images/Alamy), **78.1**; Mauritius Images, Mittenwald (Striking Images / Alamy), **17.1**; Mauritius Images, Mittenwald (Sunshine / Alamy), **13.5**; Miedzinski, Pawel, Kozieglowy/Polen, **4.8**; NASA, Washington , D.C., **54.1**; Nicolai, Axel, Sönnebüll, **12,1.3**; Norman, David, Meerbusch, **7,1.7**; Oertel, Katrin, Münster, **12,4.4**; Oser, Liliane, Hamburg, **4.9**; **40.1**; **40.2**; **40.3**; **40.4**; **40.5**; **40.6**; **40.7**; **40.8**; **40.9**; **40.10**; **40.11**; **40.12**; **44.1**; **66.1**; **72.1**; **72.2**; **73.1**; **73.2**; **73.3**; **73.4**; **73.5**; **73.6**; **76.1**; **127.1**; **127.2**; **127.3**; **127.4**; **127.5**; **127.6**; **127.7**; **127.8**; **127.9**; **12,1.5**; **5,2.1**; plainpicture GmbH & Co. KG, Hamburg (Ableimages/David Harrigan), **19.5**; plainpicture GmbH & Co. KG, Hamburg (Ableimages/Jutta Klee), **34.2**; plainpicture GmbH & Co. KG, Hamburg (amanaimages/AKIRA), **13.6**; plainpicture GmbH & Co. KG, Hamburg (AWL/Jon Arnold), **Cover.2**; plainpicture GmbH & Co. KG, Hamburg (Birgid Allig), **56.2**; plainpicture GmbH & Co. KG, Hamburg (Böhm Monika), **91.9**; plainpicture GmbH & Co. KG, Hamburg (Danel), **125.1**; plainpicture GmbH & Co. KG, Hamburg (DEEPOL by plainpicture/Susanne Kronholm), **13.2**; plainpicture GmbH & Co. KG, Hamburg (DEEPOL by plainpicture/Teo Lannie), **27.6**; plainpicture GmbH & Co. KG, Hamburg (DEEPOL/Chris Ryan), **63.4**; plainpicture GmbH & Co. KG, Hamburg (DEEPOL/David Schaffer), **30.3**; plainpicture GmbH & Co. KG, Hamburg (DEEPOL/Dinoco Greco), **84.4**; plainpicture GmbH & Co. KG, Hamburg (DEEPOL/Guerrilla), **46.5**; plainpicture GmbH & Co. KG, Hamburg (DEEPOL/Peter Muller), **99.4**; plainpicture GmbH & Co. KG, Hamburg (DEEPOL/Ramon Espelt), **28.4**; **8,1.2**; plainpicture GmbH & Co. KG, Hamburg (DEEPOL/Robert Daly),